LA ROCHEFOUCAULD

MAXIMS

TRANSLATED
WITH AN INTRODUCTION BY
Leonard Tancock

PENGUIN BOOKS

PENGUIN BOOKS

Published by the Penguin Group
Penguin Books Ltd, 27 Wrights Lane, London W8 5TZ, England
Penguin Books USA Inc., 375 Hudson Street, New York, New York 10014, USA
Penguin Books Australia Ltd, Ringwood, Victoria, Australia
Penguin Books Canada Ltd, 10 Alcorn Avenue, Toronto, Ontario, Canada M4V 3B2
Penguin Books (NZ) Ltd, 182–190 Wairau Road, Auckland 10, New Zealand

Penguin Books Ltd, Registered Offices: Harmondsworth, Middlesex, England

This translation first published 1959
9 10

Copyright © Leonard Tancock, 1959
All rights reserved

Printed in England by Clays Ltd, St Ives plc

PENGUIN CLASSICS

MAXIMS

François, duc de La Rochefoucauld, was born in 1613. In his early years he was active in the intrigues against Richelieu and later in the Fronde, but he was severely wounded in the fighting in Paris in 1652 and his political career ended in discomfiture. Thereafter he lived quietly in a small, highly intellectual society which included Mme de Sablé, Mme de Sévigné and particularly Mme de La Fayette, to whom in his later years he was united in devoted friendship. His *Mémoires* were first published in 1662 in an unauthorized and uncorrected form – the authentic version appeared only in recent times. The first Paris edition of the *Réflexions ou sentences et maximes morales*, generally known as the *Maximes*, appeared in 1665; modifications and additions were made in later editions. His *Réflexions diverses* did not appear until long after La Rochefoucauld's death in 1680.

•

La Rochefoucauld's bitter and pessimistic philosophy had a wide influence in France: the Jansenists approved it as a confirmation of their doctrine of the vileness of fallen man; Voltaire's *Candide* and the writings of Chamfort derive in part from it; Vauvenargues displays the inevitable reaction against it. Voltaire wrote that La Rochefoucauld contributed greatly to forming the taste of the nation; '*il accoutuma à penser et à renfermer ses pensées dans un tour vif, précis et délicat*'.

•

Leonard Tancock spent most of his life in or near London, apart from a year as a student in Paris, most of the Second World War in Wales and three periods in American universities as visiting professor. Until his death in 1986, he was a Fellow of University College, London, and was formerly Reader in French at the University. He prepared his first Penguin Classic in 1949 and, from that time, was extremely interested in the problems of translation, about which he wrote, lectured and gave broadcasts. His numerous translations for the Penguin Classics include Zola's *Germinal*, *Thérèse Raquin*, *The Débâcle*, *L'Assommoir* and *La Bête Humaine*; Diderot's *The Nun*, *Rameau's Nephew* and *D'Alembert's Dream*; Maupassant's *Pierre and Jean*; Marivaux's *Up from the Country*; Constant's *Adolphe*; La Rochefoucauld's *Maxims*; Voltaire's *Letters on England*; Prévost's *Manon Lescaut*; and Madame de Sévigné's *Selected Letters*.

CONTENTS

INTRODUCTION   7

PORTRAITS

Self-Portrait of the Duc de La Rochefoucauld   25
Portrait of the Duc de La Rochefaucauld
    by Cardinal de Retz   30
Portrait of Cardinal de Retz by La Rochefoucauld   32

MAXIMS

Reflections or Aphorisms and Moral Maxims   37
Posthumous Maxims   104
Maxims withdrawn by the Author   112

NOTES   126

INTRODUCTION

In his *Age of Louis XIV* Voltaire describes the *Maxims* of La Rochefoucauld as one of the works which contributed the most towards forming the taste of the French nation and giving it a feeling for aptness and precision. This little book of reflections about human nature, perhaps the most penetrating and disconcerting ever written, appeared in its original form, only about half the length of the text given here, in 1665, in the middle of the wonderful decade which saw the flowering of the genius of Molière, Racine, La Fontaine, Boileau, Bossuet, and a galaxy of masterpieces by artists in other forms, painting, sculpture, architecture, the age that is made alive for us by the incomparable letters of Mme de Sévigné, one of La Rochefoucauld's closest friends. Not that the *Maxims* were the product of a new, youthful movement in literature, for at that time the author was in his fifties, and prematurely aged by ill-health at that. They are, rather, the fruit of half a lifetime of activity and observation of others, recollected in the enforced tranquillity of middle-aged invalidism and generalized and condensed so as to be universally applicable.

François, duc de La Rochefoucauld, was born in Paris on the 15 September 1613, the eldest child of the first duke, before whom the family title for many generations had been that of Comte. His academic education was perfunctory, the usual training given to the heir of a great noble house who was destined for a military career until the moment of accession to the title, and to be married with all possible speed with a view to ensuring the succession. The Prince de Marcillac (courtesy title of the heir to the La Rochefoucauld dukedom) was married before he was fifteen to the even younger Andrée de Vivonne, a wealthy heiress who in the fullness of time bore him eight children, to whom her husband occasionally referred in letters in conventionally affectionate terms, but who seems to have played no significant part in his life. She died in about 1670.

After a baptism of fire in a military campaign in Italy the young Marcillac embarked upon the treacherous waters of court life in the thirties of the seventeenth century, and at once the curiously contradictory elements in his character began to complicate his career. One side of him was shy, contemplative, reflective, and therefore somewhat awkward and constitutionally incapable of swift decisions and ruthless action. But his self-interest, ambition, and love of intrigue drew him into all sorts of schemings usually doomed to failure because he also had strong emotional, chivalrous, and self-sacrificing urges which led him to identify himself for purely sentimental reasons with persons or groups who seemed to him unfortunate or in some way victims, and to set himself against others in influential positions whom a less quixotic and more diplomatic courtier would never have antagonized. In a word he was destined to romantic self-dedication followed by bitter disillusion.

Such was to be the pattern of the first forty years of his life. The court of Louis XIII was a hotbed of intrigue, with a weak, aloof king, the arrogant, all-powerful Richelieu, and the meddlesome queen, Anne of Austria, hated by the cardinal and disliked and avoided by her husband. Marcillac of course devoted himself to the unpopular queen, though he was to admit much later, in his *Memoirs*, that affection for her maid of honour, Mlle de Hautefort, had something to do with it. But it is true that the queen was humiliated and insulted in all sorts of ways by the cardinal and the king, and the romantic young Marcillac saw himself as a knight-errant sent to help a lady in distress. He even suggests in his *Memoirs*, though the story is not corroborated anywhere else, that at one moment in 1637 the queen's position became so intolerable that she begged him to escort her, accompanied of course by Mlle de Hautefort, to safety in Brussels. For his complicity in plots of this kind Marcillac was lucky enough to escape with only a week or two in the Bastille, followed by banishment to Verteuil, one of the family castles. After two years, however, he returned and resumed his army career.

He might have hoped that the death of the cardinal in 1642, followed by that of Louis XIII in 1643 and the assumption of the regency by Anne of Austria, would bring an improvement to his fortunes. But he found, not for the last time, that disinterested gratitude is the rarest thing in the world, for the queen mother's fair words in her time of need were now forgotten. Moreover her new first minister, Mazarin, was even more dangerous than Richelieu, being suave, indirect, feline, and treacherous. Mazarin's policies soon alienated large sections of the nobility and led to the long series of civil wars known as the Fronde. This extremely intricate period has since been glamorized by historical novelists (to say nothing of the films and TV) and at the time its events were industriously obscured by the memoirs and special pleadings of many of the participants, and no attempt can be made here to unravel the skein. From a distance it looks like a fancy-dress cavalcade of colourful personalities such as the great Condé, Mazarin, Anne of Austria, Cardinal de Retz, and Mlle de Montpensier, la grande Mademoiselle. These people galloped up and down the land, changed sides frequently (one of Mazarin's specialities was the siren-song, and every man has his price), betrayed and were betrayed, besieged and were besieged. And the bourgeoisie joined in the rush for the spoils. Whatever the political rights and wrongs, the Fronde was certainly two things. It was the last bid on the part of the old aristocracy to resist the central government of the crown, and it was a sordid struggle of self-interests, a scramble for power, position, and influence in which the foulest motives and methods were decked with labels such as duty, honour, patriotism, and glory.

Marcillac was deeply involved in all this, and once again through devotion to a woman. The Duchesse de Longueville, sister of Condé, was twenty-seven in 1646, when the liaison began, and Marcillac thirty-three. Like him, she was full of ideas of honour, heroism, and glory. She was the great love of his life and for her, during these stormy years, he set aside all thoughts of personal advantage, danger, and even common sense and, where duty to any but her was concerned, honour itself.

The end of the story is not pleasant. By 1653, after the amnesty, La Rochefoucauld (he had succeeded to the dukedom on the death of his father in 1650) found himself, at the age of forty, ruined financially, Verteuil having been razed to the ground, broken in health (for a time he had been blind as the result of an explosion), betrayed by the woman he loved, and with no hope of any public career. His experience of life had taught him that military glory is a sham, political life a jungle of careerists, religion hypocrisy or escapism, the love of women a deceit, and the motives underlying most human conduct vanity or sheer laziness. But what of friendship, simple disinterested affection, and loyalty? He discovered that there was still some to be found, for now that his active days were over and he had to retire to his country estate in order to repair his ravaged health and purse, he found real kindness from a quarter seldom credited with altruism; Gourville, a former secretary of his, who had made a fortune, was anxious to show his gratitude to his former employer. The years of solitude and bitterness were lightened by advice and even financial help gladly given by Gourville, who remained a devoted friend. It was during these years of semi-retirement in the country that La Rochefoucauld began to write his *Memoirs*, a piece of self-justification like those of so many other actors in the Fronde, but a valuable source of information not only about himself but about some of the most violent and confused years of French history.

By 1659 he managed to return to Paris, where he soon became an intimate of the circle that met in the salon of Mme de Sablé, the next great feminine influence in his life. Mme de Sablé, now nearing sixty, had been one of the group of friends who for many years had surrounded Mme de Rambouillet, until that lady's increasing infirmity and the disorganization of social life during the Fronde had broken up that famous circle. She was now living in partial retirement at the very gates of Port-Royal, the Paris headquarters of the Jansenist sect, where she divided her time between elegant social life in an environment of choice spirits such as Mme de Sévigné, Mme de La Fayette, and La Rochefoucauld, and austere piety. She and her salon had no political affinities, unlike some of the others of the time, for although Mlle de Montpensier, for example, received multitudes of friends at the Luxembourg, where the talk was mainly personal or literary, yet the fact remained that she was daughter of Gaston d'Orléans, younger brother of Louis XIII, had been the arch-fury of the Fronde, and was not very popular at the court of her young cousin Louis XIV. Mme de Sablé's salon, however, was really neutral ground, and the subjects that interested her and her friends were psychological, literary, and even linguistic, for clearness and neatness of expression were among her preoccupations. Here at last La Rochefoucauld found his true setting. At heart an observer, a speculator about human nature, a quiet witness of the human comedy and tragedy, he had spent some twenty years of his life in feverish though usually pointless and fruitless activity. His bids for fame in the military and political fields having failed, he now settled down to achieve a glorious and unique position in French literature.

The immense success of Molière's farce *Les Précieuses ridicules* and that of his later comedy *Les Femmes savantes* have for subsequent generations turned into figures of fun members of a movement that in reality was serious, civilized, and almost wholly healthy. Too often it has been forgotten that Molière was lashing with his ridicule not things themselves, but silly exaggerations of them, in this case brainless provincial copy-cats and insincere social climbers. It would be difficult to overestimate the benefits conferred by the salons upon French literature, language, and even thought during the first half of the seventeenth century, whilst some of the greatest writers of the second half had been brought up in them. In the linguistic field the constant influence of the salons of such ladies as Mme de Rambouillet and Mme de Sablé upon most of the great writers of the day gradually transformed the picturesque and over-rich legacy of the sixteenth century into the clearest and most elegant medium for conveying abstract thought known to the modern world, and in the fields of matter and taste these salons worked a comparable miracle. They turned the manners and conversation of the barrack-room into discussion of moral, sentimental, psychological problems, observation of human behaviour and speculation upon its motives and aims, overt or hidden. Of course there was some pedantry and excessive refinement, but there were also Corneille and the Pascal of the *Provinciales*.

What did the habitués of the salons talk about? Apart from the merely social and frivolous side of their activity (and the *genuine* people among them were by no means blue-stockings and pedants), their object was to enjoy interesting and elegant conversation. Now conversation means conversation, and not a series of monologues, nor impassioned argument. Therefore they avoided certain topics and cultivated others. Two subjects lead sooner or later to hot tempers, shrill monologues, rudeness, boredom, and all kinds of social discomforts: one is religion and the other politics. Moreover, apart from exhibitions of stupidity, prejudice, and intolerance, religious discussion usually ends in embarrassing personal allusions or indelicate self-revelation. Politics is not only boring to all but fanatics, but highly danger-ous in a society dominated by a tyrant and riddled with spies. In such a society these subjects are best left alone. Neither does one converse about any specialized subject on which an en-thusiastic crank can lecture in technical jargon meaningless to half the company. And above all one avoids talking about one-self, not merely because social convention discourages the first person singular, but for the much more important reason that each human being is so wrapped up in himself that he cannot abide hearing about the self of any other. A bore, somebody has said, is a fool who insists on telling you about himself when you want to tell him about yourself. For all these reasons the groups of friends who frequented the salons cultivated general topics of human behaviour in society, universal topics such as the relationships between the sexes, and in particular the plotting of the exact psychological route taken between the first inklings of interest in another person and the conscious recognition of love. For this there was no lack of textbook examples in the still universally popular *Astrée*, the interminable novel by Honoré d'Urfé, and the more recent but no less lengthy novels of Mlle de Scudéry. Such interests, and the vogue for the pen-portrait, largely due to Mlle de Scudéry's novels and now a favourite parlour game, led to the cultivation of certain literary genres suitable for discussion. One was the writing of moral portraits or 'characters' of known persons which would be circulated or read aloud, and of course the identity of the subject could not long remain unguessed in such small circles. Consequently even these personal portraits avoided stressing unpleasant characteristics, and the art consisted in combining suggestion of these and decorous attenuation without sacrificing precision. In 1659 a collection of such portraits was published, dedicated to Mlle de Montpensier, and it contained the self-portrait of La Rochefoucauld with which this translation opens. By way of an amusing contrast this is followed by an unkind portrait of La Rochefoucauld by Cardinal de Retz, published in the latter's *Mémoires*, and a malicious counter-portrait of the cardinal written immediately afterwards by La Rochefoucauld, doubtless circulated among interested parties, but not published until 1754, in an edition of the letters of Mme de Sévigné. It is noteworthy that both the indulgent self-portrait and the hostile one by Retz reveal the author of the *Maxims* as recognizably the same person.

Another genre cultivated by these people was the pithy, proverb-like generalization about human conduct known as the

sentence or *maxime*. Here, of course, the skill consists in express-
ing some thought about human motives or behaviour in a form
combining the maximum of clarity and truth with the minimum
of words arranged in the most striking and memorable order.
The concocting of these maxims was therefore a society game,
and maxims were the product of communal efforts at pruning
and arranging. The *Maxims* of La Rochefoucauld are the result
of six or seven years of patient refining during which the circle
of Mme de Sablé repeatedly offered its advice and criticism.

But generalizations, however well expressed, do not make
imperishable literary masterpieces. Had the *Maxims* been
nothing but the fruit of a clever generalizing game played by
members of a literary coterie, had they been, in a word, the work
of a committee, even though drafted by some coordinating
mind, they would not have lived for three hundred years and
remained true to the experience of us all. A work of truth and art
must have a point of view. The book of La Rochefoucauld not
only has a point of view, but it is one of the most deeply felt,
most intensely lived texts in French literature. It is one man's
experience, his likes and dislikes, sufferings and petty spites,
self-revelations and self-betrayals, regrets for past foolishness
and wisdom after the event, crystallized into absolute truths. As
he looked back upon the political jobbery of the Fronde, the self-
interest, cynicism, and treachery of all concerned, at his own
romantic and emotional excesses, his hurt pride and jealousy
over the affair of Mme de Longueville, he naturally tried to
throw the blame for events upon the falsity of others rather
than upon his own faulty judgement. The bitterness and harshness of many of the maxims, especially those about women and
the torments of love and jealousy, go far beyond the conven-
tions of a fashionable and amusing genre.

Not that the *Maxims* are merely a piece of disguised autobio-
graphy, an *apologia pro vita sua*. They also reflect certain
tendencies of the time. Modern English-speaking people, con-
ditioned by the study of one or two hackneyed 'classical' set-

books, specially selected for their suitability for middle forms and school certificate examinations, tend to think of the seventeenth-century French as heroic supermen tempered rather mysteriously by 'reason', 'will-power', 'the middle way', who lived in an age when all things were straightforward, human nature was neatly charted, and only a few obstinate and foolish cranks (labelled *attardés et égarés*) or exhibitionists (labelled *précieux*) refused to be included in the docile flock. But in reality most thinking people at that time, as always, were profoundly disturbed and perplexed by the evils and contradictions, the *grandeur et misère* of the human condition. Not only was it evident that men are neither heroes nor reasonable beings, but it was clear, as Descartes had pointed out in his *Traité des passions de l'ame* (1649), that much of man's so-called moral and psychological nature is simply the product of his physical condition, of his *humeurs*, and, more humiliating still, that man's physical condition may depend upon quite fortuitous things, devoid of any apparent sense or plan, such as the piece of grit which, according to Pascal, introduced itself into the ureter of Oliver Cromwell and reversed the trend of English history. All this is the very opposite of what the textbooks call the reason and good sense of the classical period, and these misgivings are reflected in the *Maxims*, which show mankind tossed hither and thither by passions born of a deep-seated self-centredness (*amour-propre*, *orgueil*, etc.), by all kinds of physical factors including fluctuating state of health (*les humeurs*, *le sang*, etc.), by sheer chance (*la fortune*, *le hasard*). Nor is the picture as simple as that, for if all men were actuated by *amour-propre*, passion, selfishness, ambition, or whatever it may be called, it would be fairly easy to predict their behaviour. But these things can at any moment be annulled or turned upside down by mere caprice and by the most corrosive of all human characteristics, *la paresse*, just simple laziness, apathy, the physical and moral inertia which lies at the bottom not only of all the evils but of most of the apparent virtues, since the truth is that people often cannot be bothered to do anything, good or evil. As our mid-twentieth century jargon puts it: things are done or left undone because people *couldn't care less*.

It was precisely because the French towards the middle of the seventeenth century were sickened by the iniquities of public life and frightened by these glimpses into the abyss of man's private nature that they evolved a *modus vivendi*, the ideal of the *honnête homme*. Since man cannot live unto himself, but must contrive to exist in the company of his fellow creatures, it follows that the ideal type of person is the one who can lead a sociable life with other men of all sorts and conditions, whose character, behaviour, and opinions give the least offence to others. The seventeenth-century *honnête homme* is not unlike the gentleman as defined by Cardinal Newman: 'one who never inflicts pain . . . his great concern being to make everyone at their ease and at home.' This kind of natural gentleman never hurts or embarrasses others by asserting himself or deviating too markedly from the accepted norm of decent conduct, whether in the direction of virtue or of vice, for excessive, intransigent virtue can be as painful to others as wickedness, and as upsetting to the equilibrium of society. The *honnête homme* is moderate and unobtrusive in all things, doing his exact share in society, nor more nor less. The man who insists on being different or outstanding, above all the man with a mission to 'improve' his fellow men, is either a villain or a fool, wicked or laughable. But we must not conclude from certain remarks of those uncles and brothers-in-law in Molière's plays that the *honnête homme* was a negative creature, a non-committal yes-man intent on mere conformity and etiquette, for officiousness and bowings and scrapings can be a nuisance and an embarrassment, and therefore the very opposite of good manners. Perfect manners come only from within, from real goodness, kindness, respect, and under-standing. With all this in mind the translator has usually rendered the 'untranslatable' words *honnête homme* and *honnêtes gens* by gentleman (men).

Such is the background of the *Maxims*. La Rochefoucauld gradually refined his reflections on man and his behaviour, continually submitting them for discussion to his aristocratic and literary friends, who brought to bear on them their ideals of tact and delicacy, their instinct for the exact shade of meaning in an apparently simple general statement, and their dislike of over-emphasis. Finally, in 1665, despite some argument and misgiving, particularly from some of the ladies, La Rochefoucauld decided to publish his book, to which, since this was an unclassifiable genre, he gave the comprehensive title: *Réflexions ou sentences et maximes morales*.

It was at this time that an old friendship with one of the ladies of the Sablé circle ripened into the final love of his life, a serene autumnal attachment that was to have considerable influence upon French literature. Mme de La Fayette was some twenty years younger than La Rochefoucauld, and they lived within a short distance of each other, she in the rue de Vaugirard and he in the rue de Seine. Their intimates were Mme de Sévigné, whose letters are full of their doings, Huet, La Fontaine, Ménage, and Segrais. Although she was so young Mme de La Fayette suffered from indifferent health, La Rochefoucauld was by now a chronic invalid, and as the years went by, especially after 1670 when Mme de La Rochefoucauld died and the widower became almost chair-ridden with gout, they led a tranquil, Darby and Joan existence of tender friendship. Her balance, maternal solicitude, and solid common sense did much to comfort the loneliness and bitterness of his life and to temper the harshness of subsequent editions of the *Maxims* by softening many of the statements, encouraging the full play of his more urbane, *honnête homme* instincts. Seldom, in the final edition published in his lifetime, does La Rochefoucauld fail to attenuate hurtful or unkind observations by some limiting word or phrase such as *d'ordinaire*, *d'habitude*, *la plupart des hommes*, *souvent*, *quelquefois*, some expression intended to show that he does not condemn all men out of hand, and to suggest in a gentlemanly manner that of course the reader is probably an exception. But the debt was by no means wholly on one side, for La Rochefoucauld constantly helped Mme de La Fayette in her researches into sixteenth-century history, and was always at hand to advise during the process of turning those researches into *La Princesse de Clèves*, the exquisite masterpiece which might be called the first great French novel, and which was published in 1678. La Rochefoucauld died on 17 March 1680, comforted during his last hours by Bossuet.

TEXT

The *Maxims* were the only work of La Rochefoucauld published by the author himself. There were five editions in his lifetime, published in 1665, 1666, 1671, 1675, and 1678. It is the 1678 text, the last to be corrected by the author, that is given in the standard edition in the *Grands Écrivains de la France* series, edited by D. L. Gilbert (Hachette) which has been used for this translation. The story of the additions, deletions, alterations, and changes of order made by La Rochefoucauld in these successive editions cannot be developed here, but it is of interest to note that the 1665 edition contained 317 maxims, the 1666 only 302 (he cut out some which seemed to him too indebted to the work of others, repetitions, and the magnificent long passage on *amour-propre*, No. 563 in this translation); the 1671 edition, however, contained 341, that of 1675 413, and the last, the 1678, 504. These form what might be called the 'canon', but later editors have added new maxims found in La Rochefoucauld's papers, here numbered 505 to 562, and finally there is the group numbered 563 to 641. These were withdrawn for various reasons from different editions by La Rochefoucauld, usually because he considered them clumsily expressed or too similar to others, and indeed there are some in this section which are almost exact repetitions of maxims in the main body of the work.

NOTE ON THIS TRANSLATION

La Rochefoucauld, helped by the suggestions of his friends, spent years chiselling and pruning these maxims so that they might express universally true and subtly graded facts about man's nature with such precision of meaning that they would be fully understood by all at all times. To that end the vocabulary was deliberately restricted to the smallest possible number of simple, abstract, clear words. Since local allusions, figurative language, metaphors, technical terms, in fact anything dependent upon time and place, may not be immediately clear outside a certain class of people at a certain time, such were carefully avoided, and a language evolved that was simply a precision instrument without colour, taste, or smell. Within these extremely narrow limits La Rochefoucauld, and for that matter other French classical artists, realized their aim of absolute clearness through choice between the few clear, 'foolproof' words available, and above all by taking infinite pains over *the order of those words*.

This is what makes La Rochefoucauld a challenge to the translator. In rendering into English a French prose work of a later period it is not merely permissible but desirable to manipulate words, parts of speech, the order of the various elements within a chosen unit, whether sentence or paragraph. Moreover the translator has a very wide choice between synonyms from which he can select the most appropriate word or expression from the points of view of atmosphere, stylistic suitability (heavy, light, pompous, frivolous, learned, popular, etc.), sound value, social class and character of the speaker in dialogue passages, humorous effects, and so on. And what is more, he can legitimately dress figures of speech in a different national costume, rendering, for instance, *chat en poche* by *a pig in a poke*, *bonnet blanc et blanc bonnet* by *six of one and half a dozen of the other* or *two for a pair*. But all such devices are denied to the translator of La Rochefoucauld. There is usually only one suitable word, there is usually no taste or atmosphere at all, there are not more than a handful of figurative expressions in the whole work (such as No. 507: *Tout le monde est plein de pelles qui se moquent du fourgon*, which I have ventured to transplant into *pots jeering at keettles*). But there is an economy and a word-order that must, if English syntax can possibly bear it, be respected. It would be relatively easy to translate these maxims if it were legitimate to use twice as many words, put in illustrative metaphors *ad lib.*, invent things not in the French text at all, adopt old-fashioned or quaint 'period' expressions to conceal ignorance of the exact meaning, and take no account whatever of the order, in short, forget that these are maxims and treat them as short essays. But that would be paraphrasing, which is not the same thing as translating.

I do not claim to have succeeded in this difficult piece of juggling, but I am convinced that my aim was correct. There are, of course, certain words that can scarcely be rendered by a single English word, and I have just said that to render one of La Rochefoucauld's words by a whole phrase is to betray him. Reference has already been made to *honnête homme*, which I have usually called *gentleman*. Another is *habileté*, and the difficulty here is that so often the best equivalent for La Rochefoucauld's meaning would be *savoir-vivre* or *lifemanship*, neither of which seems quite suitable as standard English. Various other words have been used. Yet another is *amour-propre*, but this is in a class by itself, for La Rochefoucauld devotes the longest of all his maxims to an attempt to define what he means by it, and he uses it all through the work like a refrain, an obsession. I have used *self-love*, or occasionally *self-interest*, and resisted the temptation to go in for elegant variation.

1959   LEONARD TANCOCK

In my struggles with the peculiar difficulties of this deceptively easy-looking text I was encouraged by many talks with the late Dr E. V. Rieu, Founder Editor of Penguin

Classics, and Dr W. G. Moore, Fellow of St John's College,
Oxford, who died last year and who was a personal friend for
over forty years. His *La Rochefoucauld: His Mind and Art*
(Oxford University Press, 1969) is the standard work on the
author in English.

Un véritable ami est le plus grand de tous les biens.

LEONARD TANCOCK

1979

PORTRAITS

SELF-PORTRAIT OF THE
DUC DE LA ROCHEFOUCAULD

I AM of medium height, well set-up and proportioned, my complexion dark but fairly uniform; my forehead is lofty and reasonably broad, eyes black, small and deep-set with thick, black but well-shaped brows. I should be hard put to it to say what sort of a nose I have, for it is neither flat nor aquiline, fleshy nor pointed – at least I do not think so – all I know is that it is big rather than small and comes down a little too low. I have a wide mouth with lips usually rather red and neither good nor bad in shape; my teeth are white and tolerably regular. I have been told that my chin is somewhat too prominent, and having just felt myself and looked in the glass to find out, I do not quite know what to make of it. As for shape of face, mine is either square or oval, but which of the two it would be very hard to say. My hair is dark and naturally wavy, thick and long enough for me to claim to have a fine crop. My expression has something melancholy and aloof about it which makes most people think I am supercilious, although I am nothing of the kind. I am very much given to movement, perhaps a bit too much, to the point of gesticulating a good deal when talking. That, in plain terms, is what I believe I am like from the outside, and I think it will be found that my own opinion of myself in this respect is not far from the truth. I will deal equally faithfully with the rest of my portrait, for I have studied myself as much as is needful for self-knowledge and am not wanting in either confidence to state freely such good qualities as I may have or candour to own up to such defects as I certainly possess. To speak first about my temperament, I am melancholic, and to such a degree that I have scarcely been seen to laugh more than three or four times in the past three or four years. Yet, I think, my melancholy would be pretty mild and easy to put up with if its only source were in my temperament, but so much depression comes from other sources and fills my imagination and dominates my mind to such an extent that most of the time I am either dreaming without uttering a word or have scarcely any conscious knowledge of what I am saying. I am very reserved with strangers and not remarkably forthcoming even with the majority of the people I know. It is a failing, I realize that, and I will leave nothing untried to cure myself, but as a certain sullen expression on my face helps to make me look even more reserved than I am, and as it is not in our power to rid ourselves of a forbidding expression due to the natural arrangement of our features, I think that when I have corrected myself within I shall still keep unfortunate signs without. I am intelligent, and I make no bones about saying so, for what is the good of being coy about it? So much beating about the bush and toning down when it is a question of stating the advantages we possess looks to me like concealing a bit of vanity behind externals of modesty, and resorting to artful wiles to make others think much better of us than we actually claim. For my part, I am content not to be thought handsomer than I make myself out to be, better humoured than I portray myself, or wittier and more sensible than I say I am. Very well then, I am intelligent, but my intelligence is spoilt by melancholy, for although I have quite a fluent tongue, a retentive memory, and am not given to muddled thinking, yet I am so preoccupied with my gloomy thoughts that I often express my ideas very badly. The conversation of well-bred people is one of the pleasures I enjoy most keenly. I like talk to be serious and mainly concerned with moral questions, but I can enjoy it when it is amusing, and if I do not throw in many little jokes myself it is at any rate not for want of appreciating the value of nicely turned frivolities or of getting much amusement out of this kind of light banter that some nimble minds can succeed in so well. If I were interested in literary glory I think that with a little trouble I could make quite a name, for I can write good prose and make up decent verse.

I am fond of all kinds of reading, but especially that in which there is something to train the mind and toughen the soul; and above all I find very great enjoyment in sharing my reading with an intelligent person, for in so doing one can continually reflect upon what is being read, and such reflections form the basis of the most delightful and profitable conversation. I can criticize quite justly works in prose or verse submitted to me, although perhaps I express my opinion a trifle too freely. Another weak point of mine is that I sometimes go in for excessively fine distinctions and over-severe criticism. I am not averse from listening to arguments, indeed I often enter into them myself, but as a rule I defend my own opinion too heatedly, and when somebody is upholding an unjust cause against me I sometimes stand up so passionately for the cause of reason that I become most unreasonable myself.

Right-thinking and naturally inclined towards good, I am so anxious to be socially acceptable that my friends could give me no greater pleasure than to point out my shortcomings in all sincerity. Those who know me at all intimately and have been kind enough to express opinions on this matter are aware that I have always welcomed such opinions with all the joy imaginable and as submissively as could be desired. My passions are all moderate and sufficiently under control: hardly ever have I been seen in a temper and I have never entertained feelings of hatred for anybody. Yet I am not incapable of taking revenge if I am wronged and it is a matter of honour not to let an insult pass unnoticed. On the contrary, I am told that my sense of duty would so effectively take over the function of hatred that I would pursue my revenge more vigorously than many another. Ambition does not worry me in the least. There are few things I fear, and death is not one of them. I am not easily touched by pity, and wish I were not at all, although there is nothing I would not do to comfort people in affliction, and indeed I believe that one should do everything, even to the point of showing great compassion for their sufferings, for misery makes people so stupid that such pity does them all the good in the world. But I also hold that one should not go beyond showing pity, and take the greatest care not to feel it oneself. This passion should have no place in a noble soul, for it only makes one soft-hearted, and it should be left to the common people, for they never do anything because of reason and have to be moved to action by their emotions.

I am fond of my friends, so fond that I would not hesitate a moment to put their interests before my own. I fit in with their wishes, patiently put up with their less agreeable moods, hasten to excuse their every act, but I do not make much show of affection, neither am I very much upset by their absence. By nature I have very little curiosity for most of the things that inspire curiosity in others. I am very secretive, and nobody could find it easier to keep to himself anything told him in confidence. Most punctilious about keeping my word, I never break it however important the matter may be, and I have made this an inviolable rule all through my life. I am scrupulously polite with women, and I do not think I have ever said a word in their presence that could have caused them embarrassment. When they are intelligent I prefer their conversation to men's, for there is a kind of smooth ease about it that is not found in us men, and moreover it seems to me that they express themselves more clearly and give a more graceful turn to what they say. I was formerly something of a ladies' man, but although I am still young that is no longer the case. I have given up making pretty compliments and am only amazed that there are so many serious-minded men who still do. I have the greatest admiration for noble passions, for they denote greatness of soul, and although the emotional stress they involve us in is hardly compatible with wise moderation, yet they are so conducive to austere virtue that they cannot rightly be condemned. Being well versed in all the delicacy and strength of deep feelings of love, I feel that if ever I fall in love it will be in this way, but knowing how I am made, I do not think this knowledge of mine will ever pass from my head to my heart.

PORTRAIT OF THE
DUC DE LA ROCHEFOUCAULD
BY CARDINAL DE RETZ

THERE has always been something baffling about everything to do with M. de La Rochefoucauld. From his earliest
days he has always insisted on dabbling in intrigue, both
when he was not concerned with petty interests, which
have never been his weak point, and when unaware of
great, which, in a different sense, have never been his
strong point. He has never been capable of any serious
business, and I do not know why this is, for he has qualities
that in anybody else would have made up for those he
lacked. He had not the necessary breadth of vision, and
indeed could not take in the whole of what was within his
range, but his good sense (and it was very good in speculation), together with his gentleness, persuasiveness, and
really admirable ease of manner, should have made up for
his lack of penetration more than they have. He has
always been chronically irresolute, but I do not even know
the cause of that, for in his case it cannot have come from
a vivid imagination, since his is anything but lively. Neither
can I attribute it to the sterility of his judgement, for,
although when it comes to action his is not outstanding,
yet he has a good supply of common sense. In a word,
the effects of this irresolution of his can be seen, although
we do not understand its cause. He has never been a real
soldier although he was extremely brave; never managed
to be a successful courtier in spite of always having had the
best intentions in that direction; never a good party man
although he has been involved in factions all his life. The

timid and diffident air you can see in his private life turned, in public affairs, into an apologetic look, for he always thought some apology was needed. And this, together with his *Maxims*, which do not show enough faith in virtue, and his behaviour, which has always followed the line of trying to get out of affairs with as much alacrity as he had displayed in getting into them, leads me to conclude that he would have been much better advised to learn to know himself and limit his efforts to proving himself, as he easily could have done, to be the most accomplished courtier of his age.

PORTRAIT OF CARDINAL DE RETZ
BY LA ROCHEFOUCAULD

PAUL de Gondi, Cardinal de Retz, is a man of great sublimity and breadth of mind, with more ostentation than true greatness of soul. He has an extraordinary memory, more forcefulness than elegance in his words, an easygoing temperament very open to influence and weak enough to bow to his friends' complaints and criticisms, little piety but some externals of religion. He looks ambitious, but is not, for vanity and the influence of others have made him undertake great things, almost always in opposition to his declared profession, and thereby he has stirred up the greatest mischief for the state without having any fixed aim to profit from it himself; and far from declaring himself the enemy of Cardinal Mazarin in order to step into his shoes, his only object was to seem to be feared by him and preen himself on the false glory of being his opponent. Nevertheless he cleverly contrived to take advantage of public troubles and become a cardinal. He suffered imprisonment courageously, and only regained his freedom through his own daring. Through sheer indolence he remained for several years in an ostentatious position of nomadic retirement. He held on to the archbishopric of Paris in defiance of Cardinal Mazarin's power, and yet after that minister's death he gave it up without realizing what he was doing and without utilizing that event in his friends' or his own interests. He has been a member of various conclaves, and has always behaved in such a way as to add to his own reputation. His natural tendency is to be idle, yet he will toil energetically when matters are pressing, only to sit back nonchalantly as soon as they are settled. He has great presence of mind, and he is so adroit at turning to his own advantage whatever opportunities fortune offers that it looks as though he had foreseen and wished for them. He loves telling tales and is so anxious to dazzle all and sundry with amazing adventures that often his imagination supplies more than his memory. Most of his qualities are bogus, and what has contributed to his renown more than anything else is his art of displaying his own defects in a flattering light. Hatred and friendship find him equally indifferent, however hard he may have tried to appear interested in one or the other. He is incapable of envy or avarice, possibly through virtue, possibly through lack of interest. He has borrowed more from his friends than any private person could hope to repay, and has made rather a point of honour of finding so much credit and undertaking to clear off the debt. He is devoid of taste and delicacy, finds everything amusing but enjoys nothing, and skilfully avoids revealing that his knowledge of everything is of the most superficial kind. The retirement he has just gone into is the most ostentatious and least genuine action in his life, a sop to his own pride disguised as piety, for he is leaving a court in which he cannot find a position, and turning his back on a world that is turning its back on him.

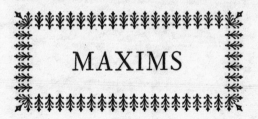

MAXIMS

REFLECTIONS OR APHORISMS
AND MORAL MAXIMS

Our virtues are usually only vices in disguise

1

What we take for virtues are often merely a collection of different acts and personal interests pieced together by chance or our own ingenuity and it is not always because of valour or chastity that men are valiant or women chaste.

2

Self-love is the greatest flatterer of all.

3

Whatever discoveries have been made in the land of self-love, many regions still remain unexplored.

4

Self-love is subtler than the subtlest man of the world.

5

We have no more say in the duration of our passions than in that of our lives.

6

Passion often makes fools of the wisest men and gives the silliest wisdom.

7

Great and glorious events which dazzle the beholder are represented by politicians as the outcome of grand designs, whereas they are usually products of temperaments and passions. Thus the war between Augustus and Antony, attributed to their ambition to seize the mastery of the world, was probably nothing more than a result of jealousy.

8

The passions are the only orators who always convince. They have a kind of natural art with infallible rules; and the most untutored man filled with passion is more persuasive than the most eloquent without.

9

The passions set aside justice and work for their own ends, and it is therefore dangerous to follow them and necessary to treat them with caution even when they seem most reasonable.

10

In the human heart new passions are for ever being born; the overthrow of one almost always means the rise of another.

11

Passions often engender their opposites. Avarice sometimes begets prodigality and prodigality avarice; a man is often resolute through weakness and bold through timidity.

12

Whatever care a man takes to veil his passions with appearances of piety and honour, they always show through.

13

Our self-esteem is more inclined to resent criticism of our tastes than of our opinions.

14

Not only do men tend to forget kindnesses and wrongs alike, but they even hate those who have done them kindnesses and give up hating those who have wronged them. The effort needed to reward goodness and take revenge upon evil seems to them a tyranny to which they are loth to submit.

15

The clemency of princes is often nothing but policy to gain popular affection.

16

This clemency, which men call a virtue, is sometimes motivated by vanity, sometimes by laziness, often by fear, and almost always by all three together.

17

The moderation of happy people comes from the tranquillity that good fortune gives to their disposition.

18

Moderation is a dread of incurring that envy and contempt which people drunk with their own success deservedly bring upon themselves; it is a pointless display of our own greatness of soul. In a word the moderation of men at the height of success is a desire to appear even greater than their destiny.

19

We all have strength enough to endure the troubles of others.

20

The steadfastness of the wise is but the art of keeping their agitation locked in their hearts.

21

Condemned men sometimes affect a steadfastness and indifference to death which is really only fear of looking death in the face; thus it can be said that this steadfastness and indifference do for their spirit what the bandage does for their eyes.

22

Philosophy easily triumphs over past ills and ills to come, but present ills triumph over philosophy.

23

Few men know death: we do not usually undergo it deliberately, but unthinkingly and out of habit, and most men die because men cannot help dying.

24

When great men succumb to long-drawn-out misfortunes they reveal that they had only borne them through strength of ambition, not of soul, and that apart from great vanity heroes are made like everybody else.

25

Greater virtues are needed to bear good fortune than bad.

26

Neither the sun nor death can be looked at steadily.

27

We often pride ourselves on even the most criminal passions, but envy is a timid and shamefaced passion we never dare acknowledge.

28

Jealousy is in some measure just and reasonable, since it merely aims at keeping something that belongs to us or we think belongs to us, whereas envy is a frenzy that cannot bear anything that belongs to others.

29

The evil we do brings less persecution and hatred upon us than our good qualities.

30

We have more strength than will-power, and when we imagine things are impossible we are trying to make excuses to ourselves.

31

If we had no faults we should not find so much enjoyment in seeing faults in others.

32

Jealousy feeds on doubts, and as soon as doubt turns into certainty it becomes a frenzy, or ceases to exist.

33

Pride always finds compensations, and even when it gives up vanity it loses nothing.

34

If we were without pride we should not object to pride in others.

35

All men have an equal share of pride; the only difference is in their ways and means of showing it.

36

It seems that nature, having so wisely arranged the organs of our bodies with a view to our happiness, has also given us pride to spare us the unpleasantness of seeing our own imperfections.

37

Pride plays a greater part than kindness in the reprimands we address to wrongdoers; we reprove them not so much to reform them as to make them believe that we are free from their faults.

38

Our promises are made in proportion to our hopes, but kept in proportion to our fears.

39

Self-interest speaks all manner of tongues and plays all manner of parts, even that of disinterestedness.

40

Self-interest blinds some, but enlightens others.

41

People too much taken up with little things usually become incapable of big ones.

42

We have not the strength to follow our reason all the way.

43

Man often thinks he is in control when he is being controlled, and while his mind is striving in one direction his heart is imperceptibly drawing him in another.

44

Strength and weakness of mind are misnomers; they are really nothing but the good or bad health of our bodily organs.

45

The vagaries of our moods are even stranger than those of fortune.

46

The attachment or indifference the philosophers felt to life was but a matter of taste on the part of their self-love, and this can no more be argued about than taste for words or choice of colours.

47

Our temperament decides the value of everything fortune bestows on us.

48

Felicity dwells in taste and not in things; we are happy through having what we enjoy, and not what others deem enjoyable.

49

We are never as fortunate or as unfortunate as we suppose.

50

People with a high opinion of their own merit make it a point of honour to be unhappy so as to convince others as well as themselves that they are worthy victims of the buffetings of fate.

51

Nothing is more certain to lower our self-satisfaction than realizing that at one moment we disapprove of what we admired at some other.

52

However diverse people's fortunes may seem, they are equalized by a certain compensation between good and bad.

53

However great may be the advantages she bestows, it is not nature alone, but nature helped by luck that makes heroes.

54

The scorn for riches displayed by the philosophers was a secret desire to recompense their own merit for the injustice of Fortune by scorning those very benefits she had denied them; it was a private way of remaining unsullied by poverty, a devious path towards the high respect they could not command by wealth.

55

Hatred of favourites is nothing but love of favour. Resentment at not enjoying it finds consolation and balm in contempt for those who do, and we withhold our own respect since we cannot deprive them of what commands that of everybody else.

56

In order to succeed in the world people do their utmost to appear successful.

57

Although men pride themselves on their noble deeds, these are seldom the outcome of a grand design but simply effects of chance.

58

Our actions seem to have lucky or unlucky stars to which they owe a great part of the praise or blame they are given.

59

No occurrences are so unfortunate that the shrewd cannot turn them to some advantage, nor so fortunate that the imprudent cannot turn them to their own disadvantage.

60

Fortune turns everything to the advantage of those she favours.

61

Men's happiness or unhappiness depends no less upon their temperament than upon fortune.

62

Sincerity is openness of heart. It is found in very few, and what is usually seen is subtle dissimulation designed to draw the confidence of others.

63

Aversion from lying is often a hidden desire to give weight to our own statements and invest our words with religious authority.

64

Truth does not do as much good in the world as the semblance of truth does evil.

65

Forethought is lauded without stint, yet it can give us no guarantee about the slightest turn of events.

66

A shrewd man has to arrange his interests in order of importance and deal with them one by one; but often our greed upsets this order and makes us run after so many things at once that through over-anxiety to have the trivial we miss the most important.

67

Simple grace is to the body what common sense is to the mind.

68

It is difficult to define love; what can be said is that in the soul it is a passion to dominate another, in the mind it is mutual understanding, whilst in the body it is simply a delicately veiled desire to possess the beloved after many rites and mysteries.

69

If pure love exists, free from the dross of our other passions, it lies hidden in the depths of our hearts and unknown even to ourselves.

70

Where love is, no disguise can hide it for long; where it is not, none can simulate it.

71

There are few people who, when their love for each other is dead, are not ashamed of that love.

72

If love be judged by most of its visible effects it looks more like hatred than friendship.

73

You can find women who have never had a love affair, but seldom women who have had only one.

74

There is only one kind of love, but there are a thousand copies, all different.

75

Love, like fire, cannot survive without continual movement, and it ceases to live as soon as it ceases to hope or fear.

76

True love is like ghostly apparitions: everybody talks about them but few have ever seen one.

77

Love lends its name to countless dealings which are attributed to it but of which it knows no more than the Doge knows what goes on in Venice.

78

In most men love of justice is only fear of suffering injustice.

79

Silence is the safest policy if you are unsure of yourself.

80

What makes us so unstable in our friendships is that it is difficult to get to know qualities of soul but easy to see those of the mind.

81

We cannot love anything except in terms of ourselves, and when we put our friends above ourselves we are only concerned with our own taste and pleasure. Yet it is only through such preference that friendship can be true and perfect.

82

Reconciliation with our enemies is nothing more than the desire to improve our position, war-weariness, or fear of some unlucky turn of events.

83

What men have called friendship is merely association, respect for each other's interests, and exchange of good offices, in fact nothing more than a business arrangement from which self-love is always out to draw some profit.

84

It is more shameful to distrust one's friends than to be deceived by them.

85

Though we often persuade ourselves that we like people more influential than ourselves, our friendship is really based on self-interest alone. We do not give them our affection for the good we want to do them but for the good we want to get out of them.

86

Suspicion on our part justifies deceit in others.

87

Social life would not last long if men were not taken in by each other.

88

Our self-esteem magnifies or minimizes the good qualities of our friends according to how pleased we are with them, and we measure their worth by the way they get on with us.

89

Everybody complains of his memory, but nobody of his judgement.

90

In daily life we are more often liked for our defects than for our qualities.

91

Even the greatest ambition, when it finds itself in a situation where its aspirations cannot possibly be realized, is hardly recognizable as such.

92

To disillusion a man convinced of his own worth is to do him as bad a turn as they did to that Athenian madman who thought all the vessels entering the harbour were his.

93

Old people are fond of giving good advice; it consoles them for no longer being capable of setting a bad example.

94

Great names debase rather than exalt those who cannot live up to them.

95

The proof of extraordinary merit is that the most envious are constrained to praise it.

96

A man's ingratitude may be less reprehensible than the motives of his benefactor.

97

Whoever said that intellect and discernment are two distinct things was mistaken. Discernment is simply a great light of the intellect which shines into the roots of things, sees everything worth noticing, and perceives things thought to be imperceptible. We must therefore agree that all the effects attributed to discernment are really produced by this broad illumination of the intellect.

98

Everybody speaks well of his own heart, but nobody dares do so of his mind.

99

Courtesy of the mind consists in thinking kind and delicate thoughts.

100

Gallantry of the mind is saying flattering things in an agreeable manner.

101

It often happens that things come into the mind in a more finished form than could have been achieved after much study.

102

The head is always fooled by the heart.

103

Not everyone who understands his own mind understands his heart.

104

There is a particular point at which men and things are in proper perspective: some must be seen close up to be well judged, but others can never be so well appreciated as from a distance.

105

The reasonable man is not the one who stumbles upon reason by chance, but the one who recognizes, understands, and savours it.

106

To be known well things must be known in detail, but as detail is almost infinite, our knowledge is always superficial and imperfect.

107

To point out that one never flirts is in itself a form of flirtation.

108

Not for long can the head impersonate the heart.

109

The tastes of youth change because it is hot-blooded; those of age remain unaltered through force of habit.

110

We give nothing so liberally as our advice.

111

The more one loves a mistress the nearer one is to hating her.

112

The flaws of the mind intensify with age, like those of the face.

113

Good marriages do exist, but not delectable ones.

114

We cannot get over being deceived by our enemies and betrayed by our friends, yet we are often content to be so treated by ourselves.

115

It is as easy to deceive ourselves without noticing it as it is hard to deceive others without their noticing.

116

Nothing is less sincere that the way people ask and give advice. The asker appears to have deferential respect for his friend's sentiments, although his sole object is to get his own approved and transfer responsibility for his conduct; whereas the giver repays with tireless and disinterested energy the confidence that has been placed in him, although most often the advice he gives is calculated to further his own interests or reputation alone.

117

The cleverest subtlety of all is knowing how to appear to fall into traps set for us; people are never caught so easily as when they are out to catch others.

118

Intention never to deceive lays us open to many a deception.

119

We are so used to disguising ourselves from others that we end by disguising ourselves from ourselves.

120

We betray more often through weakness than through deliberate intention to betray.

121

We often do good so that we can do evil with impunity.

122

When we resist our passions it is more on account of their weakness than our strength.

123

If we never flattered ourselves we should get very little pleasure indeed.

124

The really astute pretend all through their lives to eschew intrigue in order to resort to it on some special occasion and for some great purpose.

125

Habitual recourse to intrigue is the mark of a little mind, and it almost always happens that a man who uses it to cover himself on one side uncovers himself on another.

126

Intrigues and treasons simply come from lack of adroitness.

127

The surest way to be taken in is to think oneself craftier than other people.

128

Over-subtlety is false delicacy; true delicacy is sound subtlety.

129

To be slow-witted is sometimes enough to save one from a clever trickster.

130

Weakness is the only failing we cannot put right.

131

Love-making is the least of the faults of women who have given themselves up to love.

132

It is easier to be wise for others than for oneself.

133

The only good copies are those which show up the absurdity of bad originals.

134

We are never so ridiculous through qualities we have as through those we pretend to have.

135

At times we are as different from ourselves as we are from others.

136

Some people would never have fallen in love if they had never heard of love.

137

When vanity is not prompting us we have little to say.

138

We would rather run ourselves down than not talk about ourselves at all.

139

One of the reasons why so few people are to be found who seem sensible and pleasant in conversation is that almost everybody is thinking about what he wants to say himself rather than about answering clearly what is being said to him. The more clever and polite think it enough simply to put on an attentive expression, while all the time you can see in their eyes and train of thought that they are far removed from what you are saying and anxious to get back to what they want to say. They ought, on the contrary, to reflect that such keenness to please oneself is a bad way of pleasing or persuading others, and that to listen well and answer to the point is one of the most perfect qualities one can have in conversation.

140

A man of parts would often be at a loss without the company of fools.

141

We often boast that we are never bored on our own, being so conceited that we refuse to find our own company dull.

142

As the stamp of great minds is to suggest much in few words, so, contrariwise, little minds have the gift of talking a great deal and saying nothing.

143

We overpraise the qualities of others more out of satisfaction with our own opinion than respect for their merit, seeking to draw praise upon ourselves while appearing to praise them.

144

We dislike praising, and never praise anybody except out of self-interest. Praise is a subtle, concealed, and delicate form of flattery which gratifies giver and receiver in different ways: the latter accepts it as the due reward of his merit, the former bestows it so as to draw attention to his own fairness and discrimination.

145

We often make envenomed and backhanded compliments, the effect of which is to show up in those we praise faults which we dare not point out in any other way.

146

We seldom praise except to get praise back.

147

Few people are wise enough to prefer useful criticism to the sort of praise which is their undoing.

148

Some strictures can be compliments, and some compliments can be slanderous.

149

To refuse to accept praise is to want to be praised twice over.

150

Our wish to deserve the praise of others fortifies our virtue, and praise accorded to intellect, valour, and beauty encourages these things to grow.

151

It is more difficult to avoid being ruled than to rule others.

152

If we never flattered ourselves the flattery of others could do us no harm.

153

Nature provides the merit, chance calls it into play.

154

Chance cures us of many faults incurable by reason.

155

Some people are unpleasant though worthy, others pleasant despite their faults.

156

There are people whose value consists in saying and doing foolish things that serve a useful purpose, and who would upset everything if they changed their behaviour.

157

The glory of great men must always be measured against the means they have used to acquire it.

158

Flattery is a spurious coinage only made current by our vanity.

159

It is not enough to have great qualities; one must know how to manage them.

160

However glorious an action may be, it must not be deemed great unless there is a great purpose behind it.

161

If actions are to yield all the results they are capable of, there must be a certain consistency between them and one's intentions.

162

To know how to put modest talents to the best use is an art which commands admiration, and often wins a wider reputation than real worth.

163

Countless acts that seem ridiculous have hidden reasons that are exceedingly wise and sound.

164

It is easier to appear worthy of positions one does not occupy than of those one does.

165

Our real worth earns the respect of knowledgeable people, luck that of the public.

166

The world more often rewards outward signs of merit than merit itself.

167

Avarice is more opposed to good husbandry than liberality.

168

Hope may be a lying jade, but she does at any rate lead us to the end of our lives along a pleasant path.

169

We are held to our duty by laziness and timidity, but often our virtue gets all the credit.

170

It is difficult to decide whether an upright, sincere, and straightforward course of action is the outcome of probity or worldly wisdom.

171

The virtues lose themselves in self-interest like rivers in the sea.

172

If the various effects of boredom are carefully examined, it will be found that it makes us fail in our duty more often than self-interest.

173

There are various forms of curiosity: one, based on self-interest, makes us want to learn what may be useful, another, based on pride, comes from a desire to know what others don't.

174

Our minds are better employed in bearing the misfortunes that do befall us than in foreseeing those that may.

175

Constancy in love is perpetual inconstancy, inasmuch as the heart is drawn to one quality after another in the beloved, now preferring this, now that. Constancy is therefore inconstancy held in check and confined to the same object.

176

Constancy in love is of two kinds: one comes from continually finding new things to love in the beloved, and the other from making it a point of honour to remain constant.

177

Perseverance should be neither praised nor blamed, since it is only the continuance of tastes and emotions which we can neither shed nor acquire.

178

What makes us like new acquaintances is not so much weariness of the old ones or the pleasure of making a change, as displeasure at not being sufficiently admired by those who know us too well, and the hope of being more admired by those who do not yet know us well enough.

179

Irresponsible criticism of our friends is sometimes an excuse in advance for our own irresponsible conduct.

180

Repentance is not so much regret for the evil we have done as fear of the evil that may befall us as a result.

181

One kind of inconstancy comes from a fickle or shallow mind, which adopts everybody else's opinions; another, more excusable, from a feeling that nothing is worth while.

182

Vices have a place in the composition of virtues just as poisons in that of medicines: prudence blends and tempers them, utilizing them against the ills of life.

183

It is to the credit of virtue, we must admit, that men's greatest troubles are those they fall into through their misdeeds.

184

We own up to our failings so that our honesty may repair the damage those failings do us in other men's eyes.

185

Evil has its heroes as well as good.

186

We do not despise all those with vices, but we do despise all those without a single virtue.

187

The word virtue is as useful to self-interest as the vices.

188

Spiritual health is no more stable than bodily; and though we may seem unaffected by the passions we are just as liable to be carried away by them as to fall ill when in good health.

189

Nature, it seems, has the extent of each man's virtues and vices set forth in advance from the day of his birth.

190

Only the great are entitled to great faults.

191

It might be said that as we go through life the vices await us like a succession of hosts at whose houses we have to stay, and I doubt whether experience would teach us to avoid them if it were vouchsafed us to pass along the same road twice.

192

When the vices give us up we flatter ourselves that we are giving up them.

193

The sicknesses of the soul have their ups and downs like those of the body; what we take to be a cure is most often merely a respite or change of disease.

194

Defects in the soul are like wounds in the body: whatever care is taken to heal them the scars always show. Moreover they are liable to reopen at any moment.

195

What often prevents our giving ourselves up to a single vice is that we have several.

196

Our misdeeds are easily forgotten when they are known only to ourselves.

197

There are people of whom we can never believe evil without having seen it ourselves; but there are none in whom evil should surprise us when we see it.

198

We glorify the fame of some in order to debase that of others, and sometimes Monsieur le Prince and Monsieur de Turenne would not be lauded so much if people were not anxious to belittle them both.*

199

Desire to appear clever often prevents our becoming so.

200

Virtue would not go so far without vanity to bear it company.

201

The man who thinks he can find enough in himself to be able to dispense with everybody else makes a great mistake, but the man who thinks he is indispensable to others makes an even greater.

202

Would-be gentlemen disguise their failings from others and themselves; true gentlemen are perfectly aware of them and acknowledge them.

203

The true gentleman never claims superiority in anything.

204

Prudery is a sort of make-up with which women enhance their beauty.

205

The virtue of women is often love of their reputation and of a quiet life.

206

To be willing to live continuously under the eyes of gentlemen is to be a gentleman indeed.

207

Childishness follows us all the days of our life. If anybody seems wise it is only because his follies are in keeping with his age and circumstances.

208

Some silly people know themselves for what they are, and skilfully turn their silliness to good account.

209

The man who lives without folly is not as wise as he thinks.

210

Age makes men both sillier and wiser.

211

Some people are like popular songs that you only sing for a short time.

212

Most people judge men merely by their fashionable appeal, or by their fortune.

213

Love of fame, fear of disgrace, schemes for advancement, desire to make life comfortable and pleasant, and the urge to humiliate others are often at the root of the valour men hold in such high esteem.

214

For private soldiers valour is a dangerous trade they have taken up to earn their living.

215

Perfect valour and absolute cowardice are two extremes men seldom reach. Between these there lies an extensive region containing every other kind of courage, and these differ among themselves no less than faces and temperaments. There are men who freely expose themselves to danger at the beginning of an action but slacken and lose heart if it lasts long, and there are others who are content when they have satisfied the ordinary demands of honour, and do very little more. Some cannot always master their fear, whilst others are sometimes carried away by general outbreaks of panic, and yet others charge ahead because they dare not stay at their posts. Some there are whose familiarity with lesser perils strengthens their courage and prepares them to face greater. Some are brave with swords but frightened of muskets, others are confident with muskets but afraid of fighting with swords. All these different kinds of courage have this in common: darkness, by increasing fear and concealing good and bad actions alike, gives one a chance to consider one's own safety. There is yet another and more general kind of cautiousness, for no man exists who does all he would be capable of doing if he were certain of escaping with his life. It is thus clear that fear of death does take something away from valour.

216

Perfect valour consists in doing without witnesses what one would be capable of doing before the world at large.

217

Intrepidity is unusual strength of soul which raises it above the troubles, disorders, and emotions that might be stirred up in it by the sight of great danger. This is the fortitude by which heroes keep their inner peace and preserve clear use of their reason in the most terrible and overwhelming crises.

218

Hypocrisy is a tribute vice pays to virtue.

219

In time of war most men will face just enough danger to keep their honour intact, but few are prepared to go on doing so long enough to ensure the success of the enterprise for which the danger is being faced.

220

Vanity, a sense of shame, and above all temperament often enough make up the valour of men and the virtue of women.

221

Men do not want to lose their lives but they do thirst for glory: this means that the brave employ more skill and thought to avoid death than even confirmed litigators to keep hold of their property.

222

There are few people who at the first sign of age do not show in what respects their body and mind will eventually fail.

223

Gratitude is like commercial good faith: it keeps trade going, and we pay up, not because it is right to settle our account but so that people will be more willing to extend us credit.

224

Not all those who repay debts of gratitude can flatter themselves that by so doing they are being grateful.

225

The deficit in the amount of gratitude we expect for kindnesses done is due to the pride of both giver and receiver, for they fail to agree upon the value of the kindness.

226

Over-eagerness to repay a debt is in itself a kind of ingratitude.

227

Fortunate people seldom mend their ways, for when good luck crowns their misdeeds with success they think it is because they are right.

228

Pride refuses to owe, self-love to pay.

229

We have to accept respectfully the harm done us by a person whose benefactions we have enjoyed.

230

Nothing is so contagious as example, and our every really good or bad action inspires a similar one. We imitate good deeds through emulation and evil ones because of the evil of our nature which, having been held in check by shame, is now set free by example.

231

To try to be wise all on one's own is sheer folly.

232

Whatever pretext we find for our afflictions their only source is often our self-interest and vanity.

233

Afflictions give rise to various kinds of hypocrisy: in one, pretending to weep over the loss of someone dear to us we really weep for ourselves, since we miss that person's good opinion of us or deplore some curtailment of our wealth, pleasure, or position. The dead, therefore, are honoured by tears shed for the living alone. I call this a kind of hypocrisy because in afflictions of this sort we deceive ourselves. There is another hypocrisy, less innocent because aimed at the world at large: the affliction of certain persons who aspire to the glory of a beautiful, immortal sorrow. Time, the universal destroyer, has taken away the grief they really felt, but still they obstinately go on weeping, wailing, and sighing; they are acting a mournful part and striving to make all their actions prove that their distress will only end with their lives. This miserable and tiresome vanity is usually found in ambitious women, for as their sex precludes them from all the roads to glory they seek celebrity by a display of inconsolable affliction. There is yet another kind of tears that rise from shallow springs and flow or dry up at will: people shed them so as to have a reputation for being tender-hearted, so as to be pitied or wept over, or, finally, to avoid the disgrace of not weeping.

234

Those who obstinately oppose the most widely-held opinions more often do so because of pride than lack of intelligence. They find the best places in the right set already taken, and they do not want back seats.

235

We easily find consolation for the misfortunes of our friends when these give us a chance to display our fondness for them.

236

When we work for the benefit of others it would appear that our self-love is tricked by kindness and forgets itself; and yet this is the most certain way to achieve our ends, for it is lending at interest while pretending to give, in fact a way of getting everybody on our own side by subtle and delicate means.

237

Nobody deserves to be praised for goodness unless he is strong enough to be bad, for any other goodness is usually merely inertia or lack of will-power.

238

It is less dangerous to do evil to the majority of men than to do them too much good.

239

Nothing so flatters our conceit as being taken into the confidence of the great: we interpret it as a sign of our own merit instead of reflecting that most often it is simply the outcome of their vanity or inability to keep a secret.

240

Attractiveness, as distinct from beauty, may be defined as symmetry without known rules, a mysterious harmony between a person's features and between those features and the person's colouring and general bearing.

241

The instinct to flirt is fundamental to the feminine temperament, but not all women give it free rein because in some it is held in check by fear or common sense.

242

We often irritate others when we think we could not possibly do so.

243

Few things are impossible in themselves; it is not so much the means we lack as perseverance to make them succeed.

244

Supreme cleverness is knowledge of the real value of things.

245

To conceal ingenuity is ingenuity indeed.

246

What passes for generosity is often merely ambition in disguise, scorning petty interests so as to make for greater.

247

Loyalty as it is seen in most men is simply a device invented by self-love in order to attract confidence. It is a way of raising ourself above others and appointing ourselves as recipients of the weightiest matters.

248

Magnanimity despises all so as to gain all.

249

Eloquence resides no less in a person's tone of voice, expression, and general bearing than in his choice of words.

250

True eloquence consists in saying all that is required and only what is required.

251

There are people whose defects become them, and others who are ill served by their good qualities.

252

Changes of taste are as usual as changes of inclination are unusual.

253

Self-interest sets in motion virtues and vices of all kinds.

254

Humility is often merely feigned submissiveness assumed in order to subject others, an artifice of pride which stoops to conquer, and although pride has a thousand ways of transforming itself it is never so well disguised and able to take people in as when masquerading as humility.

255

Each of the emotions has its own tone of voice, gestures, and expressions, and this correspondence, good or bad, pleasant or unpleasant, is what makes people agreeable or disagreeable.

256

In every walk of life each man puts on a personality and outward appearance so as to look what he wants to be thought: in fact you might say that society is entirely made up of assumed personalities.

257

Solemnity is a mystery of the body devised to conceal flaws of the mind.

258

Good taste comes from judgement rather than from intellect.

259

The pleasure of love is loving, and we get more happiness from the passion we feel than from the passion we inspire.

260

Civility is a desire to be repaid with civility, and also to be considered well bred.

261

The training usually given to the young is a second self-love implanted in them.

262

There is no passion in which love of self rules so despotically as love, and we are always more inclined to sacrifice the loved one's tranquillity than to lose our own.

263

What is called generosity is most often just the vanity of giving, which we like more than what we give.

264

Pity is often feeling our own sufferings in those of others, a shrewd precaution against misfortunes that may befall us. We give help to others so that they have to do the same for us on similar occasions, and these kindnesses we do them are, to put it plainly, gifts we bestow on ourselves in advance.

265

Obstinacy comes from limited intelligence, and we do not readily believe what is beyond our field of vision.

266

We make a mistake if we believe that only the violent passions like ambition and love can subdue the others. Laziness, for all her languor, is nevertheless often mistress: she permeates every aim and action in life and imperceptibly eats away and destroys passions and virtues alike.

267

Readiness to believe the worst without adequate examination comes from pride and laziness: we want to find culprits but cannot be bothered to investigate the crimes.

268

In even the smallest affairs we challenge the authority of the judges, and yet we let our reputation and good name depend upon the judgement of other men, all of whom are ill disposed towards us either through jealousy, concern with their own affairs, or lack of sense. Merely in order to make them decide in our favour we imperil our peace of mind and way of life in countless ways.

269

Few men are sufficiently discerning to appreciate all the evil they do.

270

Honours won are sureties of more to be won.

271

Youth is one long intoxication: it is reason in a fever.

272

To men who have deserved high praise nothing should be more humbling than the lengths to which they will still go to get credit for petty things.

273

Some people are thought well of in society whose only good points are the vices useful in social life.

274

The charm of novelty is to love as the bloom is to fruit: it gives a lustre that is easily rubbed off and never comes back.

275

Kindliness, which is so proud of being responsive, is often choked by the most trifling self-interest.

276

Absence lessens moderate passions and intensifies great ones, as the wind blows out a candle but fans up a fire.

277

Women often think they are in love when they are not: the business of an intrigue, the emotional flutter of gallantry, natural delight in being loved, and the difficulty of saying no, all these conspire to persuade them that they are being passionate when they are merely being flirtatious.

278

The reason why we frequently criticize those who act on our behalf is that almost always they lose sight of their friends' interests in the interest of the negotiation itself, which they make their own concern for the honour and glory of having succeeded in what they have undertaken.

279

When we overstate our friends' affection for us it is as a rule not out of gratitude so much as desire to have our own worth appreciated.

280

Encouragement given to those just entering society often comes from unacknowledged envy of the well established.

281

Pride, which makes us so envious, also helps to keep envy within bounds.

282

Some disguised deceits counterfeit truth so perfectly that not to be taken in thereby would be an error of judgement.

283

Sometimes no less cleverness is needed to benefit from good advice than to think of the good advice oneself.

284

Some evil men would be less dangerous if there were no good in them at all.

285

Magnanimity is clearly enough defined by its name; nevertheless it might be said to be the common sense of pride and the noblest way to gain men's praise.

286

It is impossible to love for a second time anything you have really ceased to love.

287

It is not so much a fertile brain that enables us to find many solutions to the same problem, as lack of insight which, keeping us from going beyond what our imagination can see, prevents our discerning at first glance which solution is the best.

288

There are situations and illnesses that remedies worsen at certain times, and real wisdom consists in knowing when it is dangerous to resort to them.

289

Simplicity put on is a subtle imposture.

290

There are more flaws of temperament than of mind.

291

Men's worth, like fruit, has its season.

292

Of men's dispositions, as of most buildings, it can be said that they have different aspects, some pleasing and others not.

293

Moderation cannot take credit for combating and subjugating ambition, for the two things are never found together. Moderation is languor and idleness of the soul, ambition is its activity and energy.

294

We always like those who admire us, but not always those we admire.

295

We are far indeed from knowing all we want.

296

It is difficult to love those we do not respect, but it is no less difficult to love those whom we respect far more than ourselves.

297

The bodily humours have their normal, appointed course that imperceptibly guides and bends the will; they work together and one by one exert a mysterious influence within us. Thus, without out knowledge, they play a considerable part in all our actions.

298

Most men's gratitude is but a covert desire to receive greater gifts.

299

Almost everybody enjoys repaying small obligations, many are grateful for middling ones, but there is scarcely a soul who is not ungrateful for big ones.

300

Some follies are as catching as contagious diseases.

301

Plenty of people despise money, but few know how to give it away.

302

As a rule it is only when little is at stake that we will take a chance and not trust to appearances.

303

Whatever good we are told about ourselves, we learn nothing new.

304

We often forgive those who bore us, but we cannot forgive those who find us boring.

305

Self-interest, blamed for all our misdeeds, often deserves credit for our good actions.

306

We find few guilty of ingratitude while we are still in a position to help them.

307

A sense of one's own dignity is as admirable when kept to oneself as it is ridiculous when displayed to others.

308

Moderation has been declared a virtue so as to curb the ambition of the great and console lesser folk for their lack of fortune and merit.

309

Some men are destined to be fools, and they do foolish things not from choice but because fate herself compels them to.

310

Sometimes in life situations develop that only the half-crazy can get out of.

311

If there exist men whose ridiculous side has never been seen it is because it has never been properly looked for.

312

The reason why lovers never tire of each other's company is that the conversation is always about themselves.

313

How comes it that our memories are good enough to retain even the minutest details of what has befallen us, but not to recollect how many times we have recounted them to the same person?

314

The extreme enjoyment we find in talking about ourselves should make us fear we are not giving very much to our audience.

315

We are usually prevented from revealing our inmost thoughts to our friends by mistrust, not of them but of ourselves.

316

The weak cannot be sincere.

317

It is no great misfortune to have one's kindness repaid by ingratitude, but it is intolerable to be beholden to a scoundrel.

318

There are ways of curing madness, but none of righting the wrong-headed.

319

The proper sentiments we should feel for friends and those who have been kind to us cannot long be maintained if we consider ourselves free to discuss their defects at frequent intervals.

320

To praise princes for virtues they do not possess is to insult them without fear of the consequences.

321

We are nearer loving those who hate us than loving those who love us more than we want.

322

Only the contemptible are afraid of being treated with contempt.

323

Our wisdom is just as much at the mercy of chance as our property.

324

In jealousy there is more self-love than love.

325

Often, simply out of weakness, we get over troubles for which reason is powerless to console us.

326

To be ridiculous is more dishonouring than dishonour itself.

327

We own up to minor failings, but only so as to convince others that we have no major ones.

328

Envy is more implacable than hatred.

329

Sometimes we think we dislike flattery, but it is only the way it is done that we dislike.

330

We forgive so long as we love.

331

It is harder to be faithful to a woman when all goes well than when she is unkind.

332

Women do not realize all the implications of their coquetry.

333

In women complete unresponsiveness always goes with dislike.

334

Women are less able to curb their coquetry than their passion.

335

In love deceit almost always outstrips suspicion.

336

There is a kind of love the very excess of which excludes jealousy.

337

Certain good qualities are like the senses: people entirely lacking in them can neither perceive nor comprehend them.

338

Excessive hatred brings us down below the level of those we hate.

339

Good or bad fortune only affects us in proportion to our self-love.

340

Most women use their wits to bolster up their folly rather than their reason.

341

Salvation is scarcely more imperilled by hot-blooded youth than by lukewarm age.

342

The accent of one's birthplace persists in the mind and heart as much as in speech.

343

To achieve greatness a man must know how to turn all his chances to good account.

344

Like plants, most men have hidden properties that chance alone reveals.

345

Circumstances reveal us to others and still more to ourselves.

346

There can be no logic in a woman's mind or heart unless it is abetted by her disposition.

347

There are few sensible people, we find, except those who share our opinions.

348

When in love we often doubt what we most believe.

349

Love's supreme miracle is to cure coquetry.

350

The reason why we so bitterly resent attempts to outsmart us is that those who make them think they are cleverer than we are.

351

How hard it is to break with somebody we have ceased to love!

352

We are almost always bored by the very people by whom it is vital not to be bored.

353

A gentleman in love may behave like a madman, but not like an ass.

354

Certain flaws of character, if displayed to advantage, shine brighter than virtue itself.

355

When they die, some people are more missed than grieved over, others cause us grief but are scarcely missed.

356

As a rule we only praise unreservedly those who admire us.

357

Little minds are too much hurt by little things; great minds see all these things too, but are not hurt by them.

358

Humility is the real key to the Christian virtues, for without it we keep all our faults which pride merely conceals from others and often from ourselves.

359

Infidelities should stifle love, and we should not be jealous when we have cause to be. Only those who avoid giving cause for jealousy deserve to make us so.

360

The most trifling disloyalty to ourselves does people far more harm in our eyes than the greatest they commit to others.

361

Jealousy is always born with love, but does not always die with it.

362

Most women bewail the death of their lovers not so much because they loved them as in order to appear worthy of being loved.

363

Violence done to us often hurts less than that which we do to ourselves.

364

It is generally accepted that a man should discuss his wife as little as possible, but not generally understood that he should discuss himself even less.

365

Some good qualities degenerate into defects when they are left to nature; others, however, are never perfect when they are acquired. For example, we must use our reason to keep our wealth and counsel, but kindness and valour must be given us by nature.

366

However sceptical we may be about the sincerity of people who speak to us, we always believe they are more truthful with us than with anybody else.

367

Few virtuous women are not tired of their way of life.

368

Most virtuous women are hidden treasures, safe only because no one is looking for them.

369

The violence we do ourselves so as not to fall in love is often more of a torment than the cruelties of the person we love.

370

Few cowards always know the full extent of their fear.

371

It is almost always a lover's fault when he fails to realize he is no longer loved.

372

Most young people think they are being natural when really they are just ill-mannered and crude.

373

Often we are taken in ourselves by some of the tears with which we have deceived others.

374

The man who thinks he loves a woman for her own sake is very much mistaken.

375

Commonplace minds usually condemn whatever is beyond their powers.

376

Envy is cast out by true friendship and coquetry by true love.

377

The biggest disadvantage of a penetrating intellect is not failure to reach the goal, but going beyond it.

378

We give advice but we do not influence people's conduct.

379

As our character deteriorates, so does our taste.

380

Chance reveals virtues and vices as light reveals objects.

381

The effort we make to remain faithful to someone we love is little better than infidelity.

382

Our actions are like set rhymes: anyone can fit them in to mean what he likes.*

383

Desire to talk about ourselves and to show our failings from the viewpoint we ourselves would choose, accounts for a great deal of our candour.

384

The only thing that should astonish us is that we are still capable of astonishment.

385

A person is almost equally difficult to please when very much in love or almost cured of it.

386

No people are more often wrong than those who cannot bear to be.

387

A fool has not enough in him to make a good man.

388

Vanity may not quite overthrow the virtues, but it shakes them all to their foundations.

389

What makes the vanity of others intolerable is that it hurts our own.

390

A man will sooner give up his interests than his tastes.

391

Fortune seems never so blind as to those on whom she has nothing to bestow.

392

Fortune should be treated like health: enjoyed when good, put up with when bad, and drastic remedies should never be applied except in direst need.

393

A bourgeois air sometimes wears off in the army, but never at court.

394

You can outsmart one other person, but not all the others.

395

It is sometimes less distressing to be deceived by the person one loves than to be undeceived.

396

You can keep your first lover a long time provided you do not take a second.

397

We have not the courage to declare as a general principle that we have no shortcomings and our enemies no good qualities; but when it comes to details that is what we are none too far from believing.

398

Of all our shortcomings the one we most willingly own up to is laziness: we persuade ourselves that it is bound up with all the gentler virtues and that it merely suspends the activity of the others without wholly destroying them.

399

There is a certain dignity of manner independent of fortune, a certain distinctive air which seems to mark us out for great things. It is a value we set upon ourselves without realizing it, and by means of this quality we claim other men's deference as our due. This does more to set us above them than birth, honours, and merit itself.

400

Merit can exist without dignity, but there is no dignity without some merit.

401

Dignity is to merit what fine clothes are to natural beauty.

402

The last thing to be found in gallantry is love.

403

Fortune sometimes uses our faults for our advancement; some people are so tiresome that their merits would go unrewarded were it not that we want to get them out of the way.

404

Nature, it seems, has buried deep in our minds skill and talents of which we are unaware; the passions alone have the function of bringing them to light and thereby sometimes giving us a clearer and more comprehensive vision than ingenuity could ever do.

405

We come quite fresh to the different stages of life, and in each of them we are usually quite inexperienced, no matter how old we are.

406

Coquettish women make a point of being jealous of their admirers so as to hide their envy of other women.

407

Those who are taken in by our wiles do not seem nearly so ridiculous to us as we appear to ourselves when taken in by the wiles of others.

408

The most dangerous absurdity of elderly persons who have been attractive is to forget that they are so no longer.

409

We should often blush at our noblest deeds if the world were to see all their underlying motives.

410

The most difficult undertaking in friendship is not showing our faults to our friend, but making him see his own.

411

Almost all our failings are more pardonable than the means we employ to hide them.

412

Whatever disgrace we have brought upon ourselves, it almost always lies in our power to recover our good name.

413

Single-minded people do not please for long.

414

The crazy and the stupid can only see with their passing emotions.

415

At times our brains lead us into plain silliness.

416

The vivacity that increases with age verges on madness.

417

In love, first cured is always best cured.

418

If young women do not wish to appear coquettish, if elderly men do not wish to be ridiculous, they should never refer to love as something with which they could be personally concerned.

419

We may seem great when engaged in a task within our capacity, but in reality we often seem small in one beyond it.

420

Often we believe ourselves longsuffering in adversity when in fact we are merely prostrated, and we undergo such adversity without daring to face it, like cowards who let themselves be killed for fear of defending themselves.

421

A feeling of confidence does more for conversation than wit.

422

All the passions cause us to make mistakes, but love is responsible for the silliest ones.

423

Not many know how to be old.

424

We pride ourselves on the opposite faults to those we have; when we are weak we boast of being unyielding.

425

Perceptiveness looks like the gift of prophecy, and that flatters our vanity more than all the other qualities of the mind.

426

The charm of novelty and long habit, poles apart though they be, both prevent our realizing the shortcomings of our friends.

427

Most friends give one a distaste for friendship, and most of the pious a distaste for piety.

428

We freely forgive in our friends those faults which do not affect us.

429

Women in love forgive big indiscretions more easily than little infidelities.

430

In love's old age, as in that of life itself, we are still alive for the sufferings but no longer for the pleasures.

431

Nothing makes it so difficult to be natural as the desire to appear so.

432

To praise noble deeds unreservedly is in a sense to have a share in them.

433

The surest sign of being born with great qualities is to be born free from envy.

434

When our friends have betrayed us we owe nothing but indifference to their professions of friendship, but we should still be alive to their afflictions.

435

Chance and caprice rule the world.

436

It is easier to know man in general than to understand one man in particular.

437

A man's worth must not be judged by his great qualities, but by the use he can make of them.

438

There is a certain kind of lively gratitude which not only wipes out our debt for benefits received, but leaves our friends in our debt even when we pay them their due.

439

There are few things we should keenly desire if we really understood what we wanted.

440

The reason why friendship means little to most women is that it is insipid once they have tasted love.

441

In friendship, as in love, we are often happier because of the things we do not know than because of those we know.

442

We try to make virtues out of the faults we have no wish to correct.

443

The most violent passions sometimes let us relax, but vanity keeps us perpetually on the go.

444

Old fools are more foolish than young ones.

445

Weakness, even more than vice, is the enemy of virtue.

446

What makes the pangs of shame and jealousy so acute is that vanity cannot help us to bear them.

447

Decorum is the least important of all laws, but the best observed.*

448

It is less trouble for the right-thinking to let the wrong-headed have their way than it is to put them right.

449

When fortune takes us unawares and raises us to a high position without having led us there step by step, or without our having aspired to such a position in our dreams, it is almost impossible to hold the position securely and appear worthy of it.

450

Our pride often grows fat on what we cut from our other faults.

451

No fools are so difficult to manage as those with some brains.

452

There is no man alive who thinks each of his own qualities, in isolation, inferior to those of the man he most respects.

453

In affairs of importance a man should concentrate not so much on making opportunities as on taking advantage of those that arise.

454

There are hardly any circumstances in which we would make a bad bargain if we gave up the good said of us on condition that no evil were said either.

455

However prone the world may be to misjudge, it is nevertheless indulgent towards false merit even more often than it is unjust to genuine.

456

It is sometimes possible to be a fool with brains, but never to be a fool with discrimination.

457

It would pay us better to let ourselves be seen as we are than to try to appear what we are not.

458

Our enemies are nearer the truth in their opinion of us than we are ourselves.

459

There are several cures for love, but none of them is infallible.

460

We are very far from realizing all that our passions make us do.

461

Old age is a tyrant who prohibits all the pleasures of youth on pain of death.

462

The very pride that makes us condemn failings from which we think we are exempt leads us to despise good qualities we do not possess.

463

There is often more pride than kindness in our pity for the misfortunes of our enemies, for we make a display of sympathy in order to impress them with our own superiority.

464

There is a point beyond which good and bad fortune are too much for our emotions.

465

Innocence is very far from finding as many defenders as crime.

466

Of all the violent passions, the least unbecoming in women is love.

467

We do more distasteful things through vanity than through reason.

468

Some bad qualities make great talents.

469

We never desire passionately what we desire through reason alone.

470

All our qualities, whether good or bad, are unstable and ambiguous, and almost all are at the mercy of chance.

471

In their first affairs women are in love with their lover, later they are in love with love.

472

Pride, like the other passions, has its oddities; we are ashamed to admit we are jealous, and yet we pride ourselves on having been so and on being able to be so.

473

Rare though true love may be, true friendship is rarer still.

474

There are few women whose worth outlasts their beauty.

475

Desire for sympathy or admiration is usually the main reason for our confiding in others.

476

Our envy always lasts longer than the good fortune of those we envy.

477

The very strength of character which enables a person to fight against falling in love also makes that love violent and lasting. Weak people who are constantly tossed about by passions are hardly ever really possessed by them.

478

Imagination could never invent as many and varied contradictions as nature has put into each person's heart.

479

Only those with real strength of character can have real gentleness; those who look gentle are usually merely weak, and weakness easily goes sour.

480

Timidity is a fault that it is dangerous to censure in those we want to cure of it.

481

Nothing is rarer than genuine kindness; the very people who think they possess it are for the most part only easy-going or weak.

482

Through inertia and by force of habit the mind usually only concerns itself with what it finds easy and pleasant, and this tendency constantly sets limits to our knowledge. Nobody has ever made the effort to stretch his mind to the limit of its power.

483

We are usually spiteful more out of vanity than malice.

484

When the heart is still shaken by the remains of a passion we are more likely to yield to a fresh one than when we are quite cured.

485

Those who have known great passions remain all through their lives both glad and sorry they have recovered.

486

There are more people free from self-interest than from envy.

487

We are lazier in mind than in body.

488

Our state of mind is placid or restless not so much because of the really important happenings in our lives as because of convenient or annoying concatenations of trivial daily events.

489

However evil men may be they dare not be openly hostile to virtue, and so when they want to attack it they pretend to find it spurious, or impute crimes to it.

490

Love often leads on to ambition, but seldom does one return from ambition to love.

491

Extreme avarice almost always defeats its own object: no passion more frequently goes wide of the mark, and there is none over which the present has so much power, to the detriment of the future.

492

Avarice often produces opposite effects; countless people sacrifice all their wealth to vague and distant hopes, while others scorn great future advantages for the sake of small present gains.

493

Men seem to feel that they have not enough faults, and so they add still more to the number by certain peculiar qualities with which they affect to adorn themselves, and these they cultivate so assiduously that in the end they become natural faults beyond their power to correct.

494

The proof that men know their own weak points better than is commonly supposed is that they never make a mistake when you hear them discussing their own behaviour. The very self-love that blinds them as a rule now opens their eyes and gives them such clear vision that they omit or disguise the slightest thing that might be disapproved of.

495

Young people making their début in society should be bashful or scatterbrained, for an efficient or assured manner usually looks like impertinence.

496

Quarrels would not last long if the fault were on one side only.

497

Youth without beauty avails nothing, nor beauty without youth.

498

Some people are so shallow and frivolous that they are as far removed from having any real faults as from having any solid virtues.

499

As a rule we only take account of a woman's first love affair when she has reached her second.

500

Some people are so full of themselves that when they are in love they contrive to be taken up with the state of their own emotions instead of with the loved one.

501

Love may be delightful, but even more so are the ways in which it reveals itself.

502

Little wit with good sense is in the long run less irritating than much wit with wrongheadedness.

503

Jealousy is the greatest of all evils, and the one that inspires least pity in those who are responsible for it.

504

Having discussed the falsity of so many sham virtues, it is fitting that I should say something about the falsity of indifference to death: I mean that indifference to death that pagans pride themselves on drawing from their own strength, and not from the hope of a better life hereafter. Facing death steadfastly and being indifferent to it are not the same thing: the first is not unusual, but I do not think the second is ever genuine. Yet men have written in the most convincing manner to prove that death is no evil, and this opinion has been confirmed on a thousand celebrated occasions by the weakest of men as well as by heroes. Even so I doubt whether any sensible person has ever believed it, and the trouble men take to convince others as well as themselves that they do shows clearly that it is no easy undertaking. We may find various things in life distasteful, but we are never right to make light of death. Even those who deliberately take their own life do not count it so cheap, for they are startled when death comes by some other way than that of their own planning, and resist it as strongly as everybody else. The variations to be seen in the courage of myriads of valiant men come from the different ways their imagination presents death to them, more vividly at one time than another. Thus it comes about that after scorning what they do not know they end by fearing what they know. Unless one is prepared to consider death the direst of all evils, it should never be contemplated with all its attendant circumstances. The wisest and also the bravest are those who find the least shameful pretexts for not contemplating it, but every man capable of seeing death as it really is thinks it a fearful thing. The inevitability of death underlay all the constancy of the philosophers, who believed in travelling with a good grace along a road there was no avoiding. Not being able to prolong their own lives for ever, they stopped at nothing in order to earn eternal life for their reputation and save from the wreck whatever can be saved. So as to keep in good countenance, let us be content not to admit to ourselves all we think about it, and let us put more trust in our own character than in those feeble arguments that make out that we can draw near to death with indifference. The glory of dying with steadfast courage, the hope of being missed, the desire to leave a fair name, the assurance of being set free from the torments of life and of no longer being dependent upon the whims of fortune are remedies not lightly to be thrust aside, but neither should they be thought infallible. They offer the kind of comfort often given in war by a simple hedge to those obliged to advance towards the enemy's fire: from a distance you imagine it must provide cover, but when you come near you find it gives little help. It is illusory to suppose that death will look the same near at hand as we thought it did at a distance, and that our emotions, which are the very stuff of weakness, will be strong enough not to be daunted by the toughest of all ordeals. And we misunderstand the effects of self-love if we believe it can help us to make light of the very thing that spells its own destruction; the mind, in which we think we can find so many resources, is too feeble at such a juncture to persuade us as we would wish. On the contrary, it is the mind that most often betrays us, for instead of filling us with contempt for death it succeeds in revealing to us its hideous and terrible side, and all it can do for us is to advise us to avert our gaze and look at other things. Cato and Brutus chose glorious things to contemplate, but not so long ago a lackey was quite happy to dance on the scaffold where he was about to be broken on the wheel. And so, although motives differ, they produce the same effects, and it is therefore true that whatever differences there may be between great men and common, thousands of times men of both kinds have been seen to meet death with the same demeanour. But there has always been this distinction: in the indifference to death shown by great men their gaze is turned aside by love of glory, whilst common men are prevented from realizing the full extent of their plight by mere lack of understanding, and that leaves them free to think of something else.

505

God has put different kinds of talents in man, as he has planted different kinds of trees in nature, and so every talent, like each tree, has its peculiar properties and effects. Thus the finest pear tree in the world could not bear the commonest apples, and the most excellent talent could not produce the same effects as the most commonplace; and thus again it is as ridiculous to want to write maxims if you have not the seed within you as to expect a flower-bed to produce tulips if no bulbs have been planted.

506

It is not possible to enumerate all the kinds of vanity.

507

The world is full of pots jeering at kettles.

508

Those who overrate their own nobility are not sufficiently mindful of its origins.

509

To punish man for original sin, God has let him turn his self-love into a god to torment him in every act of his life.

510

Self-interest is the soul of self-love; hence, even as the body, cut off from its soul, is without sight, hearing, consciousness, feeling, or movement, so self-love, severed, so to speak, from its self-interest, ceases to see, hear, feel, or stir. Thus it comes about that the selfsame man who ranges over land and sea in his own interest, suddenly becomes paralysed when it comes to somebody else's. Hence the sudden languor and death we inflict upon those we talk to about ourselves, and their prompt resurrection when we bring into our story something concerning them. In a word, we notice that in conversations and business dealings, a man loses consciousness and comes back to life all in a moment according as his own interests come close or veer away.

511

As mortals we are afraid of everything, but we desire everything as though we were immortal.

512

It looks as though the devil has deliberately put laziness on the frontiers of many a virtue.

513

What makes us so prone to believe that other people have faults is the ease with which we can believe what meets our wishes.

514

The cure for jealousy is certain knowledge of what we were afraid of, for it puts an end to life or love. It is a cruel remedy, but kinder than doubt and suspicions.

515

Hope and fear are inseparable, and there is no fear without hope nor hope without fear.

516

We should not take offence when people hide the truth from us, since so often we hide it from ourselves.

517

We are often prevented from appreciating aphorisms proving the falseness of the virtues by our excessive readiness to believe that in our own case these are genuine.

518

The deference we pay to princes is a second self-love.

519

When good comes to an end it is an evil thing, and when evil does, it is good.

520

Philosophers condemn wealth only because of the bad use it is put to, and it is up to us to acquire and use it blamelessly. Then, instead of letting it feed and encourage crimes as wood keeps fire burning, we can dedicate it to all the virtues and thereby make them more beautiful and striking.

521

A neighbour's ruin is relished by friends and enemies alike.

522

Since the happiest person in the world is the one who is content with little, the great and ambitious are in this respect the most miserable, for they need innumerable good things at the same time before they can be happy.

523

Here is a convincing proof that man was not created as he now is: the more reasonable he becomes the more ashamed he is in his secret self of the unbridled wildness, unworthiness, and corruption of his feelings and inclinations.

524

The reason for so much outcry against maxims that lay bare the human heart is that people are afraid of having their own laid bare.

525

The power our loved ones have over us is almost always greater than the power we have over ourselves.

526

We are quick to criticize the faults of others, but slow to use those faults to correct our own.

527

The human condition is so wretched that while bending his every action to pander to his passions man never ceases groaning against their tyranny. He can neither accept their violence nor the violence he must do himself in order to shake off their yoke. Not only the passions but also their antidotes fill him with disgust, and he cannot be reconciled either to the discomfort of his disease or to the trouble of a cure.

528

The good and bad things that happen to us touch our emotions not in proportion to their importance but to our sensitivity.

529

Cunning is a poor substitute for sagacity.

530

We never praise except for profit.

531

The passions are merely the various whims of self-love.

532

Extreme boredom provides its own antidote.

533

Most things are praised or decried because it is fashionable to praise or decry them.

534

Many people want to be pious but few are prepared to be humble.

535

Bodily toil frees us from mental troubles, and that is what makes the poor happy.

536

Genuine self-mortification remains unknown; vanity makes any other easy to bear.

537

Humility is the altar on which God wants us to sacrifice to Him.

538

Little is needed to make a wise man happy, but nothing can content a fool. That is why nearly all men are miserable.

539

We go to far less trouble about making ourselves happy than about appearing to be so.

540

It is far easier to stifle a first desire than to satisfy all the ensuing ones.

541

Wisdom is to the soul what health is to the body.

542

As the great ones of this world are unable to bestow health of body or peace of mind, we always pay too high a price for any good they can do.

543

Before strongly desiring anything we should look carefully into the happiness of its present owner.

544

A true friend is the most precious of all possessions and the one we take least thought about acquiring.

545

Lovers do not see their mistresses' defects until the rapture is over.

546

Prudence and love are not made for each other: as love waxes, prudence wanes.

547

It is sometimes pleasant for a husband to have a jealous wife, for he constantly hears about the woman he loves.

548

How a woman is to be pitied when she has love and virtue together!

549

A wise man thinks it more advantageous not to join battle than to win.

550

It is more important to study men than books.

551

Happiness or unhappiness usually go to those who already have most of one or the other.

552

A good woman is a hidden treasure: the finder is well advised not to boast about it.

553

When we love overmuch it is hard to realize that we are no longer loved in return.

554

We only blame ourselves in order to be praised.

555

Almost always we are bored by people to whom we ourselves are boring.

556

It is never more difficult to speak well than when we are ashamed of being silent.

557

Nothing is more natural or deceptive than to believe one is loved.

558

We would rather see those we do good to than those who do good to us.

559

It is harder to disguise feelings we have than to put on those we have not.

560

Friendships taken up again need more care than friendships never dropped.

561

A man who dislikes everybody is much more unhappy than a man nobody likes.

562

For a woman hell is old age.

MAXIMS WITHDRAWN BY
THE AUTHOR

563

Self-love is love of oneself and of all things in terms of one-self; it makes men worshippers of themselves and would make them tyrants over others if fortune gave them the means. It never pauses for rest outside the self, and, like bees on flowers, only settles on outside matters in order to draw from them what suits its own requirements. Nothing is so vehement as its desires, nothing so concealed as its aims, nothing so devious as its methods; its sinuosities beggar the imagination, its transformations surpass meta-morphoses, its complications go beyond those of chemistry. No man can plumb the depths or pierce the darkness of its chasms in which, hidden from the sharpest eyes, it performs a thousand imperceptible twists and turns, and where it is often invisible even to itself and unknowingly conceives, nourishes, and brings up a vast brood of affections and hatreds. Some of these are such monstrosities that on giving them birth it either repudiates them outright or hesitates to own them. From this enveloping darkness come the ludicrous ideas it has about its own nature – the errors, ignorances, obtusenesses, and sillinesses where itself is concerned – believing, for instance, that its emotions are dead when they are merely dormant, that it has given up wanting to run just because it is resting, or that it has lost the tastes it has satiated. But this thick darkness that hides it from itself does not prevent its seeing with perfect clarity things outside itself, just as our eyes can perceive everything else and are only blind when it comes to seeing themselves. Indeed, where its main interests and really important affairs are concerned, and the violence of its desires takes up the whole of its attention, self-love sees, feels, hears, imagines, suspects, penetrates, and guesses everything, and one is tempted to believe that its every passion has magical properties of its own. Nothing is so strong and binding as its attachments, and even under the threat of the direst calamities it struggles in vain to loosen their hold. Yet sometimes, in no time and with no effort whatever, it can do things that for years on end and with the utmost exertions it had never succeeded in doing. From all this one might reasonably conclude that its desires are kindled by itself alone rather than by the beauty or value of the things desired, which are given their price and their lustre by its taste alone, and that when it pursues things that are to its liking it is running after itself, for that is really what it likes. It is made of all the opposites: domineering and obedient, sincere and deceitful, merciful and cruel, timid and daring. Its inclinations vary with the varying temperaments that bend its energies now towards glory, now riches, now pleasures. Self-love rings the changes on these according to our age, fortune, or experience, but whether it has several desires or only one is unimportant because it can spread its interest over several or concentrate upon one as need arises or as it pleases.

It is inconsistent, for apart from changes due to outside causes there are countless others arising from within itself: it is inconstant through sheer inconstancy or through shallowness, love, thirst for novelty, weariness, or satiety. It is capricious, and at times you can see it striving with the utmost eagerness and unbelievable toil to get things which are in no way advantageous and are even harmful, but which it pursues simply because it wants them. It is fantastical, and often concentrates all its energy upon the most frivolous occupations, finds pleasure in the most vapid, and can keep its pride intact while doing the most despicable things. It exists at all stages of life and at all levels, finds a living everywhere, on everything or on nothing, thrives equally well on things or on their absence, even joins forces with its declared enemies and identifies itself with their tactics and, most remarkable of all, hates itself with them, plots for its own downfall and even works to bring about its own ruin: in fine, all it cares about is existing, and provided it can go on existing it is quite prepared to be its own enemy. Hence there is nothing to be surprised at if it sometimes throws in its lot with the most rigorous austerity and brazenly joins therewith for its own destruction, for the moment of its defeat on one side is that of its recovery on another. When you think it is giving up what it enjoys it is only calling a temporary halt or ringing the changes, and at the very time when it is vanquished and you think you are rid of it, back it comes, triumphant in its own undoing.

Such is the portrait of self-love, whose whole existence is one long and incessant activity. It may fittingly be likened to the sea, the ebb and flow of whose unceasing waves is a faithful picture of the turbulent succession of its thoughts and of its eternal restlessness.

564

The passions, all of them, are nothing more than different degrees of heat and cold in the blood.

[114]

565

Moderation in times of good fortune is merely dread of the humiliating aftermath of excess, or fear of losing what one has.

566

Moderation is like sobriety: you would like to have some more, but are afraid of making yourself ill.

567

Each one of us finds in others the very faults others find in us.

568

Pride, as if weary of its own artifices and changes of face, after having played single-handed all the parts in the human comedy, puts on its natural expression and reveals itself as arrogance. Thus, strictly speaking, arrogance is the overt manifestation of pride.

569

The kind of temperament that bestows talent for small things is the opposite of the one required for great.

570

To realize how much misery we have to face is in itself a kind of happiness.

571

When you cannot find your peace in yourself it is useless to look for it elsewhere.

572

We are never as unhappy as we think, nor as happy as we had hoped.

573

Consolation for unhappiness can often be found in a certain satisfaction we get from looking unhappy.

574

We should have to be able to forecast our destiny before we could forecast our future actions.

575

How can we be answerable for what we shall want in the future, since we have no clear idea of what we want now?

576

Love is to the soul of a lover what the soul is to the body it animates.

577

As man is never free to love or cease loving, a lover has no right to complain of his mistress's inconstancy, nor she of his fickleness.

578

Justice is no more than lively fear that our belongings will be taken away from us. This is at the root of men's consideration and respect for all the interests of others, and their scrupulous care never to do them wrong. This fear keeps a man within the bounds marked out for him by his birth or fortune, and without it he would constantly be encroaching on the rights of others.

579

Justice as seen in moderate judges is but love of their high position.

580

People hate injustice not through distaste for it but because of the harm it does them.

581

When we have grown tired of loving, we are delighted at the other's unfaithfulness, for that releases us from having to be faithful.

582

The first impulse of joy we get from our friends' good luck comes neither from our kindness of heart nor from the affection we feel for them: it is an effect of self-love which holds out hopes that we may in our turn be lucky or derive some benefit from their good fortune.

583

In the adversity even of our best friends we always find something not wholly displeasing.

584

How can we expect somebody else to keep our secret if we cannot keep it ourselves?

585

The most dangerous effect of men's pride is blindness. Pride maintains and increases this blindness which prevents men from seeing the remedies that might lighten their burden and cure their faults.

586

When we give up hoping for reason in others we are at the end of our own.

587

Nobody hustles others more relentlessly than the lazy man who has indulged his own laziness and now wants to look busy.

588

We have as much right to complain about those who teach us to know ourselves as that Athenian madman who complained about the doctor for having cured him of thinking he was rich.

589

The philosophers, and Seneca above all, have not done away with men's crimes through their precepts; all they have done is to use them to build up their own pride.

590

We prove how lukewarm our own affection is when we fail to notice the cooling of that of our friends.

591

Even the wisest are wise in insignificant things but scarcely ever in their own most important affairs.

592

The subtlest wisdom can produce the subtlest folly.

593

Sobriety is concern for one's health – or limited capacity.

594

Every human talent, like every tree, has characteristics and fruits peculiar to itself.

595

We never forget things more readily than when we have wearied ourselves by talking about them.

596

The modesty that shrinks from praise is really only desire to have it more delicately expressed.

597

We never blame vice or praise virtue except through self-interest.

598

Praises bestowed on us do at least serve to keep us practising the virtues.

599

Approval given to intelligence, beauty, and valour enhances and perfects them and makes them produce finer results than they could have done by themselves.

600

Self-love sees to it that the person who flatters us is never our greatest flatterer.

601

No distinction is made between different kinds of anger, although there exists a mild and so to speak harmless kind due to hotness of blood, and another and most culpable one which is really pride gone mad.

602

Great souls are not those with fewer passions and more virtues than the ordinary run, but simply those with a stronger sense of purpose.

603

Kings turn men into coins to which they assign what value they like, and which others are obliged to accept at the official rate, and not at their real worth.

604

Fewer men are made cruel by natural ferocity than by self-love.

605

What the Italian poet has said of the virtue of women, namely that it is often simply the art of looking virtuous, can be applied to all our virtues.

606

What society calls virtue is for the most part a mere phantom conjured up by our passions; we give it a respectable name so that we can do what we like with impunity.

607

We are so biassed in our own favour that often what we take for virtues are only vices disguised by self-love.

608

Some crimes become innocent and even glorious by their sheer impudence, number, and enormity. This is why public thefts become skilful moves, and annexing provinces without justification is called making conquests.

609

If we ever admit our shortcomings it is through vanity.

610

In mankind neither good nor evil is found in excess.

611

Those who are incapable of committing great crimes do not readily suspect them in others.

612

Funereal pomp has more to do with the vanity of the living than the honouring of the dead.

613

Haphazard and infinitely varied though the world may seem, it is yet possible to make out a certain obscure interconnexion and an order fixed by Providence since time began. Thus everything proceeds in its right order and follows its own destiny.

614

Intrepidity is needed to uphold a man's courage in conspiracies, whereas bravery alone gives him all the strength of purpose he needs in the perils of war.

615

Those who would define victory by her family tree might be tempted, like the poets, to call her the daughter of heaven, for her origin is not of this world. In reality victory is the sum total of a multitude of deeds which, far from having her as their object, are motivated solely by the personal interests of the doers, since all the individuals who make up an army, by working each for his own glory and advancement, combine to produce such a great and general benefit.

616

No man can answer for his courage if he has never been in peril.

617

We are more inclined to set limits to our gratitude than to our hopes and desires.

618

Imitation is always unfortunate, and anything artificial is displeasing through those very qualities that are delightful in the original.

619

We do not always regret the loss of our friends because of their worth, but because of our own needs and the flattering opinion they had of us.

620

It is very hard to distinguish between kindness to all and sundry, and consummate cleverness.

621

We cannot be good all the time unless others believe they can never do us harm with impunity.

622

To feel confident of pleasing is often a way of being thoroughly displeasing.

623

We do not readily believe what is beyond our field of vision.

624

Self-confidence is at the root of most of our confidence in others.

625

Fashions of thought, as well as the fortunes of the world, come round on the whirligig of time.

626

The foundation and reason of perfection and beauty is truth. Nothing whatsoever can be beautiful and perfect if it is not truly everything it should be and if it has not everything it should have.

627

Some beautiful things are more impressive when left imperfect than when too highly finished.

628

Magnanimity is a noble effort of pride which, by this effort, makes a man master of himself so as to be master of all things.

629

Luxury and excessive refinement are sure forerunners of the decadence of states, because when all individuals seek their own interests they neglect the public weal.

630

Of all our passions the least well understood by ourselves is laziness. It is the most violent and malignant of all, though its violence is imperceptible and its ravages exceedingly difficult to see. If we carefully examine its power we shall see that in every eventuality it takes over the mastery of our emotions, interests and pleasures. It is the *remora*, which has the strength to bring the mightiest ships to a standstill, the calm that is more dangerous to important affairs than breakers and the fiercest tempests. The tranquillity of laziness casts a secret spell over the soul that suddenly puts a stop to the most relentless pursuits and brings to nought the most unbreakable resolutions. In conclusion, this passion can best be described by saying that laziness is as it were a blissful state of the soul that consoles it for every loss and is welcomed as a substitute for every good.

631

Men make virtues out of various acts thrown together by mere chance.

632

We enjoy seeing through others, but not being seen through.

633

To safeguard one's health at the cost of too strict a diet is a tiresome illness indeed.

634

It is easier to fall in love when you are out of it than to get out of it when you are in.

635

Most women yield through weakness rather than passion, and that is why as a rule enterprising men are more successful than others although no more attractive.

636

To be lukewarm in love oneself is a sure way of inspiring love.

637

The candour lovers require of each other so as to be sure when each has ceased to love the other is wanted less as a warning that soon they will no longer be loved than as a reassurance that they are still loved when nothing is said to the contrary.

638

Love may most aptly be compared with a fever, for we have no more power over the one than the other, either in its violence or duration.

639

The cleverest course for the not so clever is to know when to accept the wise guidance of others.

640

We are always nervous of seeing the person we love if we have just been flirting with somebody else.

641

If we are strong enough to own up to our misdeeds we must not fret about them.

NOTES

Maxim 198. Monsieur le Prince was the courtesy title of the great Condé. He and Turenne were commanders, first on the same side and then on opposite sides, during the wars of the Fronde.

Maxim 382. *Nos actions sont comme les bouts-rimés, que chacun fait rapporter à ce qu'il lui plaît.* A literary game consisted of giving *bouts-rimés* (sets of rhyming words, e.g. *cœur, sœur; femme, flamme;* etc.) on which one had to construct poems.

Maxim 447. The *Grands Écrivains* text gives *La bienfaisance est la moindre de toutes les lois, et la plus suivie.* But many early editions give *La bienséance* etc. I have followed the latter reading since 'decorum' seems to me to make better sense than 'charity', 'philanthropy', etc.

READ MORE IN PENGUIN

In every corner of the world, on every subject under the sun, Penguin represents quality and variety – the very best in publishing today.

For complete information about books available from Penguin – including Puffins, Penguin Classics and Arkana – and how to order them, write to us at the appropriate address below. Please note that for copyright reasons the selection of books varies from country to country.

In the United Kingdom: Please write to *Dept. JC, Penguin Books Ltd, FREEPOST, West Drayton, Middlesex UB7 OBR*

If you have any difficulty in obtaining a title, please send your order with the correct money, plus ten per cent for postage and packaging, to *PO Box No. 11, West Drayton, Middlesex UB7 OBR*

In the United States: Please write to *Penguin USA Inc., 375 Hudson Street, New York, NY 10014*

In Canada: Please write to *Penguin Books Canada Ltd, 10 Alcorn Avenue, Suite 300, Toronto, Ontario M4V 3B2*

In Australia: Please write to *Penguin Books Australia Ltd, 487 Maroondah Highway, Ringwood, Victoria 3134*

In New Zealand: Please write to *Penguin Books (NZ) Ltd,182–190 Wairau Road, Private Bag, Takapuna, Auckland 9*

In India: Please write to *Penguin Books India Pvt Ltd, 706 Eros Apartments, 56 Nehru Place, New Delhi 110 019*

In the Netherlands: Please write to *Penguin Books Netherlands B.V., Keizersgracht 231 NL–1016 DV Amsterdam*

In Germany: Please write to *Penguin Books Deutschland GmbH, Friedrichstrasse 10–12, W–6000 Frankfurt/Main 1*

In Spain: Please write to *Penguin Books S. A., C. San Bernardo 117–6° E–28015 Madrid*

In Italy: Please write to *Penguin Italia s.r.l., Via Felice Casati 20, I–20124 Milano*

In France: Please write to *Penguin France S. A., 17 rue Lejeune, F–31000 Toulouse*

In Japan: Please write to *Penguin Books Japan, Ishikiribashi Building, 2–5–4, Suido, Tokyo 112*

In Greece: Please write to *Penguin Hellas Ltd, Dimocritou 3, GR–106 71 Athens*

In South Africa: Please write to *Longman Penguin Southern Africa (Pty) Ltd, Private Bag X08, Bertsham 2013*

READ MORE IN PENGUIN

A CHOICE OF CLASSICS

Honoré de Balzac	**The Black Sheep**
	The Chouans
	Cousin Bette
	Eugénie Grandet
	A Harlot High and Low
	Lost Illusions
	A Murky Business
	Old Goriot
	Selected Short Stories
	Ursule Mirouet
	The Wild Ass's Skin
Marquis de Custine	**Letters from Russia**
Corneille	**The Cid/Cinna/The Theatrical Illusion**
Alphonse Daudet	**Letters from My Windmill**
René Descartes	**Discourse on Method and Other Writings**
Denis Diderot	**Jacques the Fatalist**
	Nun
	Rameau's Nephew and **D'Alembert's Dream**
Gustave Flaubert	**Bouvard and Pecuchet**
	Madame Bovary
	The Sentimental Education
	The Temptation of St Anthony
	Three Tales
Victor Hugo	**Les Misérables**
	Notre-Dame of Paris
Laclos	**Les Liaisons Dangereuses**
La Fontaine	**Selected Fables**
Madame de Lafàyette	**The Princesse de Clèves**
Lautrémont	**Maldoror** and **Poems**